Mini
CROCHET

Mini
CROCHET

TEENY TINY TREASURES TO MAKE AND SHARE

CATHERINE HIRST

CICO BOOKS

This edition published in 2026 by CICO Books
An imprint of Ryland Peters & Small Ltd
20–21 Jockey's Fields, London WC1R 4BW
www.rylandpeters.com
Email: euregulations@rylandpeters.com

10 9 8 7 6 5 4 3 2 1

Text © Catherine Hirst 2012, 2026
Design, photography and illustration © CICO Books 2012,
2026

A CIP catalogue record for this book is available from the
British Library.

ISBN: 978-1-80065-641-3

Printed in China

Managing editor: Gillian Haslam
Editor: Marie Clayton
Pattern checker: Susan Horan
Design concept: Luis Peral Aranda
Designers: Elizabeth Healey and Paul Stradling
Photographer: Geoff Dann
Stylist and set designer: Trina Dalziel

Assistant editor: Danielle Rawlings
Art director: Sally Powell
Creative director: Leslie Harrington
Head of production: Patricia Harrington
Publishing manager: Carmel Edmonds

The authorised representative in the EEA is
Authorised Rep Compliance Ltd.,
Ground Floor. 71 Lower Baggot Street,
Dublin, D01 P593, Ireland
www.arccompliance.com

**Safety note: Make sure to keep the projects away
from babies and small children as they are tiny enough
to swallow.**

Contents

Introduction

I have always loved small things. When I was a little girl, my uncle made me a dolls' house, and I spent many happy hours rearranging the furniture and dolls that lived inside, making up stories about their lives. So to create these projects in miniature was a labour of love for me! The projects in this book are meant to inspire the imagination in the same way – from Gus the Dachshund chasing lizards on the farm where he lives, to the Russian doll sisters living in their onion dome in St Petersburg. Children will love playing with these pieces and creating their lives, and many of the projects make lovely gifts for the young or young-at-heart! Don't give them to babies or very small children though, as many items are tiny enough to swallow.

The very tiny crochet hooks used for the projects are steel hooks, which come in smaller sizes than aluminium hooks. If you've never used small hooks and thin crochet cotton, it may take some patience until it feels natural. Try to loosen your tension – if you make tiny stitches too tight, you won't be able to insert your hook.

Many projects do not have exact yarn amounts specified because such a tiny amount was used it was almost impossible to measure. Suffice it to say that I didn't finish a single skein of yarn while making the projects in this book, even using the same colours for many different projects. There are three main sizes of yarn used:
- No.8 crochet cotton: this is the thinnest yarn used (the larger the number, the thinner the yarn), for the very tiny pieces and requires some getting used to. A few projects are crocheted with embroidery thread, which is about the same thickness.
- No.5 crochet cotton: I used this for the majority of the projects; it's a manageable size and because most crochet cotton is mercerised and so slightly shiny, it gives a lovely sheen to the projects and makes them look very neat. I can highly recommend DMC Petra No.5 cotton, which is lovely and silky to work with.
- Baby (4-ply) yarn and sock yarn: these yarns are used with a smaller hook than usual to make the tight stitches needed.

Throughout the book I have given the yarn weight allowing you to make substitutions. You can scale these projects up by using a larger yarn and hook if desired, but remember to use a smaller hook than usual for the yarn for a tight tension.

Stuff the projects firmly, but do not overstuff or you will pull the stitches apart and the stuffing will show through. Crochet cotton is much easier to stuff firmly because cotton is not elastic so the stitches will not tend to stretch as much; be more careful about overstuffing when you are using either the 4-ply yarn or the sock yarn.

Most of the projects in this book are made using the spiral method, so the ends of rounds are not joined with a slip stitch. Use a stitch marker to mark the first stitch of each round – I used a very small safety pin slipped through the stitch because a larger stitch marker would get in the way. Any projects not made with the spiral method are clearly noted in the pattern, including the slip stitch and chain 1 needed for the joined method. Almost all the projects start with a magic circle. This method of beginning a 3-D crochet project is brilliant because it results in no hole whatsoever in the top of the piece. If you've never used the magic circle method before, you can find clear instructions in the Basic Techniques section on page 123. You could also look online for video tutorials of the technique.

Using safety eyes or embroidering eyes is essential if you are giving the item to a young child. If the recipient is an adult (or yourself!) you can insert the safety eyes at the end without putting on the backs – they will stay in place once inserted.

I had a wonderful time creating these projects and I know you will too. Happy crocheting!

CHAPTER 1

Flying Friends

From the tiniest ducks you have ever seen to wee owls, robins and butterflies, this chapter is all about our sweet winged friends. Why not make a pair of lovebirds to show someone you really care? Or perch some robins on your kitchen windowsill to remind you that spring is just around the corner? There's even a nest pattern included so your flying friends can have their own little home.

Mama AND Baby Bird

Mama Fuzzy Bird spoils her Baby Bird; she feeds him only the very choicest worms, and makes sure their nest is always clean, cosy and warm. She likes to snuggle up to his fuzzy little head at night and tell him long stories about all the creatures who live in their forest. Baby Bird can't wait to explore the big, wide world.

MAMA BIRD
BODY
Make 6dc in magic circle, pull tail to close.
Rnd 1: 2dc in each dc. (12 sts)
Rnd 2: *1dc in next dc, 2dc in next dc; rep from * to end. (18 sts)
Rnd 3: *1dc in each of next 2 dc, 2dc in next dc; rep from * to end. (24 sts)
Rnd 4: *1dc in each of next 3 dc, 2dc in next dc; rep from * to end. (30 sts)
Rnd 5: *1dc in each of next 4 dc, 2dc in next dc; rep from * to end. (36 sts)
Rnds 6–11: 1dc in each dc. (36 sts)
Rnd 12: *1dc in each of next 4 dc, dc2tog; rep from * to end. (30 sts)
Rnd 13: *1dc in each of next 3 dc, dc2tog; rep from * to end. (24 sts)
Rnd 14: *1dc in each of next 2 dc, dc2tog; rep from * to end. (18 sts)
Rnd 15: *1dc in next dc, dc2tog; rep from * to end. (12 sts)
   Turn inside out. Attach safety eyes. Stuff firmly.
Rnd 16: Dc2tog around. (6 sts)
   Fasten off, leaving a long tail. Weave through rem sts and pull tight to close.

ABBREVIATIONS
dc: double crochet
dc2tog: double crochet 2 together decrease. Insert hook in next st, yrh, pull through a loop. Without finishing st, insert hook in next st, yrh and pull through a loop. Yrh and pull through all three loops on hook
rem: remaining
rep: repeat
Rnd(s): round, rounds
ss: slip stitch
st(s): stitch, stitches
yrh: yarn round hook

MATERIALS
Birds
- ½ x ball, approx 20m (22yds), of No.8 crochet cotton, such as DMC Perle No.8 100% cotton, in pale green
- ⅛ x ball, approx 26m (28½ yds), of laceweight yarn, such Rowan Kidsilk Haze 70% mohair/30% silk, in pale green
- 1.5mm (US size 8) steel crochet hook
- 2 x pairs 6mm (¼ in.) safety eyes
- Toy stuffing
- Sewing needle
- Small piece orange felt
- Fabric/craft glue

Nest
- ⅛ x 50g ball, approx 26m (28½ yds), of No.5 crochet cotton, such as DMC Petra No.5 100% cotton, in beige
- 2.0mm (US size 4) steel crochet hook

FINISHED SIZES

Mama bird: 4cm (1½ in.) long
Baby bird: 2.5cm (1 in.) long
Nest: 6cm (2⅓ in.) diameter

NOTES
Use one strand of each yarn held together throughout – both birds were made with less than one ball of each. After making each piece, turn inside out – the reverse side will be fuzzier. You will need to turn the main body inside out before making the final decreases.

WINGS (MAKE 2)

Make 6dc in magic circle, pull tail to close.

Rnd 1: 2dc in each dc. (12 sts)

Rnd 2: 2dc in each dc. (24 sts)

Rnd 3: *1dc in next dc, 2dc in next dc; rep from * to end. (36 sts)

Fasten off, leaving a long tail.

BABY BIRD

BODY

Make 6dc in magic circle, pull tail to close.

Rnd 1: 2dc in each dc. (12 sts)

Rnd 2: *1dc in next dc, 2dc in next dc; rep from * to end. (18 sts)

Rnd 3: *1dc in each of next 2 dc, 2dc in next dc; rep from * to end. (24 sts)

Rnds 4–9: 1dc in each dc. (24 sts)

Rnd 10: *1dc in each of next 2 dc, dc2tog; rep from * to end. (18 sts)

Rnd 11: *1dc in next dc, dc2tog; rep from * to end. (12 sts)

Turn inside out. Attach safety eyes. Stuff firmly.

Rnd 12: Dc2tog around. (6 sts)

Fasten off, leaving a long tail. Weave through rem sts and pull tight to close.

WINGS (MAKE 2)

Make 6dc in magic circle, pull tail to close.

Rnd 1: 2dc in each dc. (12 sts)

Rnd 2: 2dc in each dc. (24 sts)

Fasten off, leaving a long tail.

FINISHING

Fold each wing in half to make a half-moon shape. Sew flat side of each wing to either side of body. Cut a triangle of orange felt for beak and attach with fabric or craft glue.

BIRD'S NEST

Make 6dc in magic circle, pull tail to close.

Rnd 1: 2dc in each dc. (12 sts)

Rnd 2: *1dc in next dc, 2dc in next dc; rep from * around. (18 sts)

Rnd 3: *1dc in each of next 2 dc, 2dc in next dc; rep from * around. (24 sts)

Rnd 4: *1dc in each of next 3 dc, 2dc in next dc; rep from * around. (30 sts)

Rnd 5: *1dc in each of next 4 dc, 2dc in next dc; rep from * around. (36 sts)

Rnd 6: *1dc in each of next 5 dc, 2dc in next dc; rep from * around. (42 sts)

Rnd 7: *1dc in each of next 6 dc, 2dc in next dc; rep from * around. (48 sts)

Rnd 8: *1dc in each of next 7 dc, 2dc in next dc; rep from * around. (54 sts)

Rnds 9–13: 1dc in each dc. (54 sts)

Ss in next st, fasten off.

FINISHING

Weave in ends.

NOTES

Both the birds and the nest are made in continuous spiral rounds, so you will not join with a slip stitch. Use a stitch marker to mark the first stitch of each round throughout. You could also use the nest pattern to make a tiny bowl to hold small items such as earrings or coins.

Wise LITTLE Owls

Twit twoo! These two little owls, Sunshine and Snowy, have such big eyes because they go hunting for tasty mice late at night when all the other birds are asleep. They are very wise and like to read histories and adventure stories.

OWL

Make 6dc in magic circle; pull tail to close circle.
Rnd 1: 2dc in each dc. (12 sts)
Rnd 2: *1dc in next dc, 2dc in next dc; rep from * to end. (18 sts)
Rnd 3: *1dc in each of next 2 dc, 2dc in next dc; rep from * to end. (24 sts)
Rnds 4–11: 1dc in each dc. (24 sts)
    Fasten off.

WINGS (MAKE 2)

Make 5dc in magic circle. Pull tail to make half-moon shape.
Row 1: Ch1, 1dc in each dc across.
    Fasten off, leaving a long tail.

FINISHING

Cut two circles of cream or yellow felt, push a safety eye through the centre of each and attach to head. Stitch edges of felt circles in place with running st.
Stuff owl. Press two halves of open top of owl together so eyes are at front. Join yarn to dc at side, work ears and join both thicknesses: 3ch, 1tr in next st, 1htr in next st, 1dc in each of next 2 sts, ss in each of next 2 sts, 1dc in each of next 2 sts, 1htr in next st, 1tr in each of last 2 sts. Fasten off.
Sew flat side of wings to sides of body.
Cut a small triangle from orange felt and glue below eyes for beak.

ABBREVIATIONS

ch: chain
dc: double crochet
htr: half treble
rep: repeat
Rnd(s): round, rounds
ss: slip stitch
st(s): stitch, stitches
tr: treble

MATERIALS

- Oddments of No.5 crochet cotton, such as DMC Petra No.5 100% cotton, in white or yellow
- 1.5mm (US size 8) steel crochet hook
- Cream or yellow felt
- 1 x pair safety eyes for each owl
- Sewing needle
- Toy stuffing
- Orange felt
- Craft/fabric glue

FINISHED SIZES

Owl: 3cm (1¼ in.) tall

Beautiful Butterflies

Colourful butterflies flit from flower to flower, looking so lovely... these little gems can be made into hair ornaments, used to adorn a garment, or even attached to a rod and inserted into the soil of a houseplant. The only limit is your imagination!

BUTTERFLY WINGS (MAKE 2 FOR EACH BUTTERFLY)

Using B, ch8, ss in first ch to form lp for lower wing.

Rnd 1: Ch12, ss in first ch to form lp for upper wing.

Rnd 2: Ch1, 10dc in lower wing lp, ss between lps, 14dc in upper wing lp, join with ss in first dc.
Fasten off.
Using C, join into any dc.

Rnd 3: *1dc in first dc, 2dc in next dc; rep from * around, while slip stitching in ss. Ss in first dc to close. (36 dc)

Rnd 4: Ss in each of next 3 dc, *ch2, ss in same dc as last ss (picot made), ss in each of next 2 dc; rep from * 12 times, ch2, ss in same dc as last ss, ss in each of last 6 dc, join with ss in first ss.
Fasten off.

FINISHING

Place two flat edges of wings together. Join A to first ss after last picot on lower wing, working through both pieces, work dc down flat edges to first picot on upper wing (for tail), ch4 (for head), miss first ch, dc in next 3 ch. 1dc in each dc of joining row, then ch4 (for tail), miss first ch, ss in next 3 ch, ss in each dc to last 3 dc.
Fasten off.
Cut a length of A and pull through top of butterfly head with hook to form antennae; make a knot in each end, then trim just above knot.

FLOWER

Ch4, join with ss to form ring.

Rnd 1: Ch3, 11tr in ring, join with ss in top of first ch-3.

Rnd 2: Ch1, *ch4, miss next tr, 1dc in next tr; rep from * ending 4ch, miss last tr, ss in first ch to join.

Rnd 3: *Ss in next ch-4 sp, [ch3, 3tr, ch3, ss] all in same sp; rep from * to end.
Fasten off.

FINISHING

Weave in ends.

MATERIALS

Butterflies
- Small amounts of No.5 crochet cotton, such as DMC Petra No.5 100% cotton, in green (A)
- Oddments of No.5 crochet cotton, such as DMC Petra No.5 100% cotton, in at least two other colours (B) and (C)
- 1.5mm (US size 8) steel crochet hook

Flowers
- Small amount of 4-ply (baby) yarn, such as King Cole Merino Blend 4-ply 100% wool, in various colours
- 2.0mm (US size 4) steel crochet hook

FINISHED SIZES

Butterfly: 4.5cm (1¾ in.) long
Flower: 4.5cm (1¾ in.) diameter

Robin Red Breast

When the robins start building their nests in the garden, spring has definitely arrived! With their distinctive red breasts, these tiny robins will make you smile – make a whole family to brighten up your life. And everyone needs a cosy home, so why not make the little nest as well to hold the robin family?

ABBREVIATIONS

ch(s): chain, chains
dc: double crochet
dc2tog: double crochet 2 together decrease. Insert hook in next st, yrh, pull through a loop. Without finishing st, insert hook in next st, yrh and pull through a loop. Yrh and pull through all three loops on hook
htr: half treble
rep: repeat
Rnd(s): round, rounds
ss: slip stitch
st(s): stitch, stitches
tr: treble
yrh: yarn round hook

MATERIALS

Robin
- Small amount of DK (light worsted) weight pure wool in beige (A) and red (B)
- 3.5mm (US size 00) steel crochet hook
- 1 x pair 6mm (¼ in.) safety eyes
- Toy stuffing
- Sewing needle
- Small piece of orange felt
- Craft glue

Nest
- ¼ x 50g ball, approx 26m (28½ yds), of DK (light worsted) weight pure wool in beige (A)
- 2.5mm (US size 2) steel crochet hook
- Sewing needle

ROBIN

BODY

Using A, make 6dc in magic circle, pull tail to close.
Rnd 1: 2dc in each dc. (12 sts)
Rnd 2: *1dc in next dc, 2dc in next dc; rep from * to end. (18 sts)
Rnds 3–6: 1dc in each dc. (18 sts)
Rnd 7: *1dc in next dc, dc2tog; rep from * to end. (12 sts)
Insert safety eyes and secure. Stuff firmly.
Rnd 8: Dc2tog around. (6 sts)
Fasten off, leaving a long tail.

RED BREAST

Using B, make 6dc in magic circle, pull tail to close.
Rnd 1: 2dc in each dc. (12 sts)
Rnd 2: *1dc in next dc, 2 dc in next dc; rep from * to end. (18 sts)
Ss in next stitch, fasten off, leaving a long tail.

WINGS (MAKE 2)

In magic circle, ch2 and make 5htr; pull tail to half-moon shape.
Fasten off, leaving a long tail.

TAIL

Ch5, [4tr, ss] in fourth ch from hook, ss in next ch, ch3, [4tr, ss] in same ch.
Fasten off, leaving a long tail.

FINISHING

Use yarn end to sew hole in body closed.
Sew breast, wings and tail to body using yarn ends.
Cut a small triangle of orange felt for the beak and glue below eyes.

NEST

Make 6dc in magic circle, pull tail to close.

Rnd 1: 2dc in each dc. (12 sts)

Rnd 2: *1dc in next dc, 2dc in next dc; rep from * around. (18 sts)

Rnd 3: *1dc in each of next 2 dc, 2dc in next dc; rep from * around. (24 sts)

Rnd 4: *1dc in each of next 3 dc, 2dc in next dc; rep from * around. (30 sts)

Rnd 5: *1dc in each of next 4 dc, 2dc in next dc; rep from * around. (36 sts)

Rnd 6: *1dc in each of next 5 dc, 2dc in next dc; rep from * around. (42 sts)

Rnd 7: *1dc in each of next 6 dc, 2dc in next dc; rep from * around. (48 sts)

Rnd 8: *1dc in each of next 7 dc, 2dc in next dc; rep from * around. (54 sts)

Rnds 9–13: 1dc in each dc. (54 sts)
Ss in next st, fasten off.

FINISHING

Weave in ends.

FINISHED SIZES

Robin: 3cm (1¼ in.) tall, 4cm (1½ in.) across
Nest: 7cm (2¾ in.) diameter

Teeny Ducks ON A POND

Quack! Matilda, Stella and Bonnie are three ducks who all live together in a small pond. They eat lots of algae, insects and small fish and sometimes they find a particularly choice frog. They spend the rest of their time quacking to each other about their ducklings and all the goings-on in the pond.

DUCK
BODY
Using A and 1.4mm (US size 9) hook, make 6dc in magic circle, pull tail to close.

Rnd 1: 2dc in each dc. (12 sts)

Rnd 2: *1dc in next dc, 2dc in next dc; rep from * to end. (18 sts)

Rnds 3–5: 1dc in each of next 3 sts, 1htr in each of next 2 sts, 1tr in each of next 2 sts, 1htr in each of next 2 sts, 1dc in each of next 3 sts, 1htr in next st, 1tr in each of next 2 sts, 1htr in next st, 1dc in each of next 2 sts. (18 sts)

Rnd 6: 1dc in each of next 3 sts, htr2tog, tr2tog, htr2tog, dc in each of next 9 sts. (15 sts)
Stuff firmly.

Rnd 7: 1dc in each of next 3 sts, [dc2tog] 3 times, 1dc in next st, [dc2tog] twice, 1dc in next st. (10 sts)
Ss in next st. Fasten off, leaving a long tail.

ABBREVIATIONS
dc: double crochet

dc2tog: double crochet 2 together decrease. Insert hook in next st, yrh, pull through a loop. Without finishing st, insert hook in next st, yrh and pull through a loop. Yrh and pull through all three loops on hook

htr: half treble

htr2tog: half treble 2 together decrease. *Yrh, insert hook into first st, yrh, pull through a loop. Without finishing st, rep from * into next st. Yrh and pull yarn through all five loops on hook

rep: repeat

Rnd(s): round, rounds

ss: slip stitch

st(s): stitch, stitches

tr: treble

tr2tog: treble 2 together decrease. *Yrh, insert hook into first st, yrh, pull through a loop, yrh and pull yarn through first two loops on hook. Without finishing st, rep from * into next st. Yrh and pull yarn through all three loops on hook

yrh: yarn round hook

MATERIALS
Ducks
• ¼ x ball, approx 10m (11 yds), of No.8 crochet cotton, such as DMC Perle No.8 100% cotton, in yellow (A)
• 1.4mm (US size 9) steel crochet hook
• Oddment of 6-strand embroidery thread in orange, split into 3 strands (B)
• Oddment of 6-strand embroidery thread in black
• Toy stuffing
• Sewing needle

Pond
• Small amount of No.5 crochet cotton, such as DMC Petra No.5 100% cotton, in blue (C)
• 1.5mm (US size 8) steel crochet hook

HEAD

Using A and 1.4mm (US size 9) hook, make 6dc in magic
  circle, pull tail to close.
Rnd 1: 2dc in each dc. (12 sts)
Rnds 2–4: 1dc in each dc. (12 sts)
  Stuff head.
Rnd 5: Dc2tog around. (6 sts)
  Fasten off, leaving a long tail.

BEAK

Using B and 1.4mm (US size 9) hook, make 6dc in magic
  circle. Pull tail to make half-moon shape.

FINISHING

Use yarn end to close hole in duck body. Use yarn end to sew
  head to body. Sew flat side of beak to head. Embroider
  eyes on either side of head using black embroidery thread.

POND

Using C and 1.5mm (US size 8) hook, make 6dc in magic
  circle, pull tail to close.
Rnd 1: 2dc in each dc. (12 sts)
Rnd 2: *1dc in next dc, 2dc in next dc; rep from * to end.
  (18 sts)
Rnd 3: *1dc in each of next 2 dc, 2dc in next dc; rep from
  * to end. (24 sts)
Rnd 4: *1dc in each of next 3 dc, 2dc in next dc; rep from
  * to end. (30 sts)
Rnd 5: *1dc in each of next 4 dc, 2dc in next dc; rep from
  * to end. (36 sts)
Rnd 6: *1dc in each of next 5 dc, 2dc in next dc; rep from
  * to end. (42 sts)
Rnd 7: *1dc in each of next 6 dc, 2dc in next dc; rep from
  * to end. (48 sts)
Rnd 8: Ss in next st, *ch3, miss 1 st, ss in next st; rep from
  * to end.
  Fasten off.

FINISHING

Weave in ends.

Lovable Lovebirds

Little birds in love: is there anything sweeter? These tiny lovebirds could be used stand-alone, attached to hair ornaments or used as buttons, or why not thread a ribbon through the top and hang them from a miniature tree or potted plant? Wherever you use them, they will bring a little love and happiness.

LOVEBIRD

Make 6dc in magic circle; pull tail to close.

Rnd 1: 2dc in each dc. (12 sts)

Rnd 2: *1dc in next dc, 2dc in next dc; rep from * to end. (18 sts)

Rnd 3: *1dc in each of next 2 dc, 2dc in next dc; rep from * to end. (24 sts)

Rnds 4–8: 1dc in each dc. (24 sts)

Rnd 9: *1dc in each of next 2 dc, dc2tog; rep from * to end. (18 sts)

Rnd 10: *1dc in next dc, dc2tog; rep from * to end. (12 sts)

Stuff lightly and flatten sphere to disc shape.

Rnd 11: Dc2tog around. (6 sts)

Fasten off, leaving a long tail.

FINISHING

Use yarn end to close hole in lovebird.

Cut two heart shapes from red felt and attach one on each side as wings using glue. Cut diamond shape from orange felt, fold in half and sew to front of disc for beak.

Embroider eyes using 3 strands of the black embroidery thread.

ABBREVIATIONS

dc: double crochet

dc2tog: double crochet 2 together decrease. Insert hook in next st, yrh, pull through a loop. Without finishing st, insert hook in next st, yrh and pull through a loop. Yrh and pull through all three loops on hook

rep: repeat

Rnd(s): round, rounds

st(s): stitch, stitches

yrh: yarn round hook

MATERIALS

- Small amount of No.5 crochet cotton, such as DMC Petra No.5 100% cotton, in white
- 1.5mm (US size 8) steel crochet hook
- Toy stuffing
- Sewing needle
- Small pieces of red and orange felt
- Oddment of 6-strand cotton embroidery thread in black, split into 3 strands
- Craft/fabric glue

FINISHED SIZES

Lovebird: 2.5cm (1 in.) diameter

CHAPTER 2

Furry Friends

Everybody loves little animals... and there's a project just for you in this chapter, whether your furry favourite is a dog, a cat or even a fuzzy sheep. You can have fun making the accessories that really make the projects complete – apples for the little piggies, the fish for Harry the cat, and of course a tasty bone for Gus the sausage dog!

THE *Three Bears*

Mama Bear wants to make sure her family is warm and cosy during their long hibernation, so she's spent winter evenings crocheting blankets for all three of them. This pattern requires less sewing up because the head and body of the bear are made in one piece.

ABBREVIATIONS

beg: beginning
ch: chain
cont: continue
dc: double crochet
dc2tog: double crochet 2 together decrease. Insert hook in next st, yrh, pull through a loop. Without finishing st, insert hook in next st, yrh and pull through a loop. Yrh and pull through all three loops on hook
htr: half treble
rem: remaining
rep: repeat
Rnd(s): round, rounds
sp: space
ss: slip stitch
st(s): stitch, stitches
yrh: yarn round hook
tr: treble

MATERIALS

Papa Bear
• ⅟₁₆ x ball, approx 41m (45 yds), of 4-ply (fingering) cotton yarn, such as Patons 4 ply 100% cotton, in green (MC)
• Small amount of 4-ply (fingering) wool, such as King Cole Merino Blend 4-ply 100% wool, in blue (CC)
• 2.0mm (US size 4) steel crochet hook

Mama Bear
• ⅟₁₆ x ball, approx 34m (37 yds), of 4-ply (fingering) cotton yarn, such as Rowan Summerlite 4-ply 100% cotton, in pink (MC)
• Small amount of 4-ply (fingering) wool, such as King Cole Merino Blend 4-ply 100% wool, in pink (CC)
• 2.0mm (US size 4) steel crochet hook

Baby Bear
• Small amount of No.8 crochet cotton, such as DMC Cotton Perle No.8 100% cotton, in purple (MC)
• Small amount of No.8 crochet cotton, such as DMC Perle No.8 100% cotton, in cream (CC)
• 1.4mm (US size 9) steel crochet hook

All bears
• Toy stuffing
• Embroidery thread in red and blue
• Sewing needle

Striped and Granny Square Blankets
• Oddments of No.8 crochet cotton, such as DMC Perle No.8 100% cotton, in various colours
• 1.5mm (US size 8) steel crochet hook
• Yarn needle

Rose Square Blanket
• Oddments of No.8 crochet cotton, such as DMC Perle No.8 100% cotton, in pink (A) and cream (B)
• 1.4mm (US size 9) steel crochet hook
• Yarn needle

NOTES

All bears are made with the same pattern; Baby Bear is made with a smaller hook and finer yarn to make him smaller overall.

If you want to use safety eyes, add them before stuffing the head.

The bear head and body are made in one piece in continuous spiral rounds, so you will not join with a slip stitch. Use a stitch marker throughout to mark the first stitch of each round.

BEARS

HEAD/BODY

Using MC, make 6dc in magic circle and pull tail to close.

Rnd 1: 2dc in each dc. (12 sts)

Rnd 2: *1dc in next dc, 2dc in next dc; rep from * to end. (18 sts)

Rnd 3: *1dc in each of next 2 dc, 2dc in next dc; rep from * to end. (24 sts)

Rnd 4: *1dc in each of next 3 dc, 2dc in next dc; rep from * to end. (30 sts)

Rnd 5: 1dc in each dc. (30 sts)

Rnd 6: *1dc in each of next 3 dc, dc2tog; rep from * to end. (24 sts)

Rnd 7: *1dc in each of next 2 dc, dc2tog; rep from * to end. (18 sts)

Rnd 8: *1dc in next dc, dc2tog; rep from * to end. (12 sts)
Stuff firmly.

Rnd 9: Dc2tog around. (6 sts)

Begin making body:

Rnd 10: 2dc in each dc. (12 sts)

Rnd 11: *1dc in next dc, 2dc in next dc; rep from * to end. (18 sts)

Rnd 12: *1dc in each of next 2 dc, 2dc in next dc; rep from * to end. (24 sts)

Rnds 13–16: 1 dc in each dc. (24 sts)

Rnd 17: *1dc in each of next 2 dc, dc2tog; rep from * to end. (18 sts)

Rnd 18: *1dc in next dc, dc2tog; rep from * to end. (12 sts)
Stuff firmly. If more stuffing in head is desired, use non-hook end of a larger crochet hook to push stuffing up into head.

Rnd 19: Dc2tog around. (6 sts)
Cut yarn, leaving a long tail. Thread through rem sts and pull tight to close.

EARS (MAKE 2)

Using MC, make 6dc in magic circle. Pull tail to make half circle.
Fasten off, leaving a tail for sewing.

ARMS (MAKE 2)

Using MC, make 6dc in magic circle and pull tail to close.

Rnd 1: *1dc in next dc, 2dc in next dc; rep from * to end. (9 sts)

Rnd 2: 1dc in each dc. (9 sts)

Rnd 3: *1dc in next dc, dc2tog; rep from * to end. (6 sts)

Cont making 1dc in each dc (no need to use a stitch marker) until arms are desired length (teddies shown have 3 rounds). When desired length is reached, ss in next st, then fasten off, leaving a long tail.

FINISHED SIZES

Papa/Mama bears: 8cm (3⅛ in.) tall

Baby bear: 5cm (2 in.) tall

Striped blanket: 6 x 5cm (2⅓ x 2 in.) (See overleaf)

Rose square blanket: 5 x 5cm (2 x 2 in.) (See overleaf)

Granny square blanket: 4.5 x 4.5cm (1¾ x 1¾ in.) (See overleaf)

LEGS (MAKE 2)

Using CC, make 8dc in magic circle and pull tail to close.

Rnd 1: *1dc in next dc, 2dc in next dc; rep from * to end. (12 sts)

Change to MC.

Rnd 2: 1dc in each dc. (12 sts)

Rnd 3: *1dc in next dc, dc2tog; rep from * to end. (8 sts)

Cont making 1dc in each dc (no need to use a stitch marker) until legs are desired length (teddies shown have 3 rounds). When desired length is reached, ss in next st, then finish off, leaving a long tail.

FINISHING

Sew ears to head with flat side facing head. Curl slightly toward front of face. Stuff arms and legs if desired (tail of yarn can be stuffed inside and used as padding).

Sew arms and legs to body.

Embroider nose and mouth using red embroidery thread. Embroider French knots in blue embroidery thread for eyes.

BLANKETS

STRIPED BLANKET FOR PAPA BEAR

Change colour every other row throughout.

Using 1.5mm (US size 8) hook, ch 21.

Row 1: Miss first ch, 1dc in each dc, turn. (20 sts)

Row 2: 1dc in each dc, turn.

Rep Row 2 another 20 times.

To make border, attach new colour and dc in each dc, making 16 dc down each side, ch1 before turning each corner.

Fasten off, weave in all ends.

ROSE SQUARE BLANKET FOR MAMA BEAR (MAKE 4 SQUARES)

Using A and 1.4mm (US size 9) hook, ch4, join with ss to form a ring.

Rnd 1: 8dc in ring.

Rnd 2: *ch4, miss 1 dc, 1dc in next dc; rep from * to end, ss in base of first ch-4 to join.

Rnd 3: *ss in next ch-4 sp, [1dc, 1htr, 1dc] in same sp; rep from * to end.

Rnd 4: *ss between two petals, ch6; rep from * to end, ss in first ss to join.

Change to B.

Rnd 5: Join in any ch-6 sp and ch3, [2tr, ch2, 3tr] in same sp, ch1. *In next ch-6 sp, [3tr, ch2, 3tr], ch 1. Rep from * to end; ss in top of first ch-3 to join.

Using A, join squares with dc.

Using A, dc around edge of entire blanket.

Fasten off, weave in ends.

GRANNY SQUARE BLANKET FOR BABY BEAR (MAKE 4 SQUARES)

Change colour each round.

Using 1.5mm (US size 8) hook, ch4, join with ss to form a ring.

Rnd 1: Ch2, 2htr in ring, *ch2, 3htr in ring; rep from * twice, ch2, ss in top of first 2-ch to join.

Join new colour in any 2-ch corner sp.

Rnd 2: Ch2, 2htr in corner sp, ch2, 3htr in same corner sp, *ch1, 3htr in next corner sp, ch2, 3htr in same corner sp; rep from * twice, ch1, ss in top of first 2-ch to join.

With new colour, join 4 squares using dc.

Using same colour, work *1dc in each st to corner, [1dc, ch1, 1dc] in corner sp; rep from * around blanket, ss in first dc. Fasten off, weave in ends.

FINISHING

Press blankets gently.

Fifi AND THE STRIPEY BALL

Fifi's stripey ball is almost as big as she is... she loves to chase after it and try to bite it, but it's too big for her mouth. But soon Fifi will grow and the ball won't, so she will succeed!

PUPPY

HEAD
Using A and 1.0mm (US size 12) hook, make 6dc in magic circle, pull tail to close.
Rnd 1: 2dc in each dc. (12 sts)
Rnd 2: *1dc in next dc, 2dc in next dc; rep from * to end. (18 sts)
Rnd 3: *1dc in each of next 2 dc, 2dc in next dc; rep from * to end. (24 sts)
Rnds 4–8: 1dc in each dc. (24 sts)
Rnd 9: *1dc in each of next 2 dc, dc2tog; rep from * to end. (18 sts)
Rnd 10: *1dc in next dc, dc2tog; rep from * to end. (12 sts)
Stuff firmly.
Rnd 11: Dc2tog around. (6 sts)
Fasten off, leaving a long tail.

MUZZLE
Using A and 1.0mm (US size 12) hook, make 12dc in magic circle, pull tail to close.
Rnds 1–2: 1dc in each dc. (12 sts)
Fasten off, leaving a long tail.

EARS (MAKE 2)
Using A and 1.0mm (US size 12) hook, and starting with a long tail, ch4.
Row 1: Miss 1 ch, 1dc in each of next 3 chs, turn. (3 sts)
Row 2: Ch1, 1dc in each dc, turn. (3 sts)
Row 3: Ch1, 1dc in first dc, 1htr in next dc, [1dc, ss] in last dc.
Fasten off.

ABBREVIATIONS
ch(s): chain, chains
dc: double crochet
dc2tog: double crochet 2 together decrease. Insert hook in next st, yrh, pull through a loop. Without finishing st, insert hook in next st, yrh and pull through a loop. Yrh and pull through all three loops on hook
htr: half treble
rep: repeat
Rnd(s): round, rounds
ss: slip stitch
st(s): stitch, stitches
yrh: yarn round hook

MATERIALS
Puppy
• Small amount of laceweight yarn, such Rowan Kidsilk Haze 70% mohair/30% silk, in pink (A)
• 1.0mm (US size 12) steel crochet hook
• Toy stuffing
• Oddment of 6-strand embroidery thread in black and pink
• Sewing needle
• 10cm (4 in.) narrow pink ribbon

Ball
• Oddments of No.5 crochet cotton, such as DMC Petra No.5 100% cotton, in desired colours (B)
• 1.5mm (US size 8) steel crochet hook
• Toy stuffing
• Sewing needle

FINISHED SIZES

Puppy: 3.5cm (1⅜ in.) long, 2.5cm (1 in.) high
Ball: 2.5cm (1 in.) diameter

BODY

Using A and 1.0mm (US size 12) hook, make 6dc in magic
    circle, pull tail to close.
Rnd 1: 2dc in each dc. (12 sts)
Rnd 2: *1dc in next dc, 2dc in next dc; rep from * to end.
    (18 sts)
Rnd 3: *1dc in each of next 2 dc, 2dc in next dc; rep from *
    to end. (24 sts)
Rnds 4–13: 1dc in each dc. (24 sts)
Rnd 14: *1dc in each of next 2 dc, dc2tog; rep from * to end.
    (18 sts)
Rnd 15: *1dc in next dc, dc2tog; rep from * to end. (12 sts)
    Stuff firmly.
Rnd 16: Dc2tog around. (6 sts)
    Do not fasten off. To make tail, with yarn still attached to
    body, ch10, miss 1 ch, 1dc in each ch.
    Fasten off.

LEGS (MAKE 4)

Using A and 1.0mm (US size 12) hook, make 4dc in magic
    circle, pull tail to close.
Rnds 1–5: 1dc in each dc. (4 sts)
    Fasten off, leaving a long tail.

FINISHING

Use yarn end to close hole in head, then sew head on body.
    Sew ears to head. Sew legs to body.
Embroider nose on muzzle in black embroidery thread then
    sew muzzle to front of head. Embroider eyes on head using
    black thread.
Wrap pink ribbon around neck for collar and use pink
    embroidery thread to work a round of running stitch along
    centre of ribbon.

STRIPEY BALL

Change colour every 2 rnds throughout.
Using B and 1.5mm (US size 8) hook, make 6dc in magic
    circle, pull tail to close.
Rnd 1: 2dc in each dc. (12 sts)
Rnd 2: *1dc in next dc, 2dc in next dc; rep from * to end.
    (18 sts)
Rnd 3: *1dc in each of next 2 dc, 2dc in next dc; rep from * to
    end. (24 sts)
Rnds 4–7: 1dc in each dc. (24 sts)
Rnd 8: *1dc in each of next 2 dc, dc2tog; rep from * to end.
    (18 sts)
Rnd 9: *1dc in next dc, dc2tog; rep from * to end. (12 sts)
    Stuff firmly.
Rnd 10: Dc2tog around. (6 sts)
    Fasten off, leaving a long tail.

FINISHING

Use yarn end to close hole in ball.

Gus THE Sausage Dog

Gus the Dachshund is a happy fellow; he loves to chase lizards and snooze in the sunshine on the farm where he lives, and he loves chewing on his pink bone. Self-striping sock yarn means making Gus colourful is easy.

DOG

HEAD

Using A and 2.0mm (US size 4) hook, make 6dc in magic circle, pull tail to close.

Rnd 1: 2dc in each dc. (12 sts)

Rnd 2: *1dc in next dc, 2dc in next dc; rep from * to end. (18 sts)

Rnds 3–6: 1dc in each dc. (18 sts)

Rnd 7: *1dc in next dc, dc2tog; rep from * to end. (12 sts)
Insert safety eyes and secure. Stuff firmly.

Rnd 8: Dc2tog around. (6 sts)
Fasten off, leaving a long tail. Leave bottom open.

MUZZLE

Using A and 2.0mm (US size 4) hook, make 4dc in magic circle, pull tail to close.

Rnd 1: 1dc in each dc. (4 sts)

Rnd 2: *1dc in next dc, 2dc in next dc; rep from * once more. (6 sts)

Rnd 3: 1dc in each dc. (6 sts)
Fasten off, leaving a long tail.

EARS (MAKE 2)

Using A and 2.0mm (US size 4) hook, and starting with a long tail, ch4.

Row 1: Miss 1 ch, 1dc in each of next 3 chs, turn. (3 sts)

Row 2: Ch1, 1dc in each dc, turn.

Row 3: Ch1, 1dc in first dc, 1htr in next dc, [1dc, ss] in last dc.
Fasten off.

ABBREVIATIONS

beg: beginning

cont: continue

ch(s): chain, chains

dc: double crochet

dc2tog: double crochet 2 together decrease. Insert hook in next st, yrh, pull through a loop. Without finishing st, insert hook in next st, yrh and pull through a loop. Yrh and pull through all three loops on hook

htr: half treble

rep: repeat

Rnd(s): round, rounds

ss: slip stitch

st(s): stitch, stitches

yrh: yarn round hook

MATERIALS

Dog

- Small amount of self-striping 4-ply (fingering) sock yarn, such as Regia Magic Mirror Color 75% Wool/25% Polyamide (A)
- 2.0mm (US size 4) steel crochet hook
- Toy stuffing
- 1 x pair 6mm (¼ in.) safety eyes
- Black embroidery thread
- Sewing needle

Bone

- Small amount of No.8 crochet cotton, such as DMC Perle No.8 100% cotton, in pink (B)
- 1.0mm (US size 12) steel crochet hook
- Sewing needle

Striped blanket

- Small amount of 4-ply (fingering) wool, such as King Cole Merino Blend 4-ply 100% wool, in purple, blue and cream
- 2.0mm (US size 4) steel crochet hook

BODY

Using A and 2.0mm (US size 4) hook, make 6dc in magic circle, pull tail to close.

Rnd 1: 2dc in each dc. (12 sts)

Rnds 2–13: 1dc in each dc. (12 sts)
Stuff firmly.

Rnd 14: Dc2tog around. (6 sts)
Fasten off, leaving a long tail.

LEGS (MAKE 4)

Using A and 2.0mm (US size 4) hook, make 6dc in magic circle, pull tail to close.

Rnds 1–3: 1dc in each dc. (6 sts)
Fasten off, leaving a long tail.

TAIL

Using A and 2.0mm (US size 4) hook, make 4dc in magic circle, pull tail to close.

Rnds 1–3: 1dc in each dc. (4 sts)
Fasten off, leaving a long tail.

FINISHING

Embroider nose on muzzle using black embroidery thread, then sew muzzle to head.

Sew ears to head.

Sew rem hole in body closed.

Sew head, legs and tail to body.

BONE (MAKE 2 HALVES)

Using B and 1.0mm (US size 12) hook, make 6dc in magic circle, pull tail to close.

Rnd 1: 2dc in each dc. (12 sts)
Ss in next st, fasten off.

Work a second piece as first to end of Round 1. Holding first circle next to new circle, begin working 1dc in each dc of first circle around, and then all the way around new circle, so they are joined. 1dc in each dc all the way around both circles again. (24 sts)

Dc2tog all the way around both circles.

Next rnd: [1dc in next dc, dc2tog] 4 times. (8 sts)

Work 3 rounds in dc.
Fasten off leaving a long tail.
Stuff bone end.

FINISHING

Sew both halves of bone together.

FINISHED SIZES

Dog: 7.5cm (3 in.) from nose to tip of tail, 4cm (1½ in.) high
Bone: 2.5cm (1 in.) long, 1.5cm (⅔ in.) wide
Striped blanket: 6.5 x 5.5cm (2½ x 2³⁄₁₆ in.)

STRIPED BLANKET

Change colour every 2 rows throughout.

Using 2.0mm (US size 4) hook, ch 21.

Row 1: Miss first ch, 1dc in each ch to end, turn. (20 sts)

Row 2: Ch1, 1dc in each dc to end, turn. (20 sts)

Rows 3–20: As Row 2.
Fasten off.

FINISHING

Weave in ends. Press gently.

Harry the Cat GOES FISHING

Here, kitty, kitty! Harry the cat can always be tempted by a delicious fish, which is why you have to keep him away from the aquarium. Harry also enjoys playing with a bit of string or a feather on a stick. But his favourite thing is curling up on the lap of a warm human.

CAT
BODY AND HEAD
Using A, make 6dc in magic circle, pull tail to close.

Rnd 1: 2dc in each dc. (12 sts)

Rnd 2: *1dc in next dc, 2dc in next dc; rep from * to end. (18 sts)

Rnd 3: *1dc in each of next 2 dc, 2dc in next dc; rep from * to end. (24 sts)

Rnds 4–8: 1dc in each dc. (24 sts)

Rnd 9: Dc2tog around. (12 sts)
Stuff firmly.

Rnds 10–13: 1dc in each dc. (12 sts)

Rnd 14: Dc2tog around. (6 sts)
Fasten off, leaving a long tail.

EARS (MAKE 2)
Using A, ch3.

Row 1: Miss first ch, 1dc in next 2 chs, turn.

Row 2: Ch1, dc2tog.
Fasten off, leaving a long tail.

TAIL
Using A, ch4.

Row 1: Miss first ch, 1dc in next 3 chs, turn.

Row 2: Ch1, 1dc in each of 3 dc, turn. Change to B, alternate colours every two rows.

Rows 3–10: Ch1, dc in each dc, turn.

Row 11: Ch2, 1htr in each dc, ss in top of ch-2.
Fasten off, leaving a long tail.

FINISHING
Use yarn end to close hole in cat head. Sew ears to head and tail to body, curving it around.

Cut two small felt triangles and glue to front of ears. Cut a smaller felt triangle and glue to centre of face for nose.

Embroider French knots for eyes in green thread and stitch whiskers in black thread.

FISH
BODY (MAKE 2 HALVES)
Using C, ch2.

Row 1: Miss first ch, 1dc in next ch, turn.

Row 2: Ch1, 2dc in dc, turn.

Row 3: Ch1, 2dc in each dc to end, turn.

ABBREVIATIONS
dc: double crochet

dc2tog: double crochet 2 together decrease. Insert hook in next st, yrh, pull through a loop. Without finishing st, insert hook in next st, yrh and pull through a loop. Yrh and pull through all three loops on hook

htr: half treble

rep: repeat

Rnd(s): round, rounds

ss: slip stitch

st(s): stitch, stitches

yrh: yarn round hook

MATERIALS
- Small amounts of No.5 crochet cotton, such as DMC Petra No.5 100% cotton, in blue (A), white (B) and peach (C)
- 1.5mm (US size 8) steel crochet hook
- Toy stuffing
- Oddments of 6-strand cotton embroidery thread, in black and green
- Sewing needle
- Small piece of pink felt
- Craft/fabric glue

FINISHED SIZES

Cat: 4.5cm (1¾ in.) tall
Fish: 3cm (1¼ in.) long

Rows 4–5: Ch1, 1dc in each dc to end, turn.
Row 6: Ch1, [dc2tog] twice, turn.
Row 7: Ch1, dc2tog.
  Fasten off.

FINS (MAKE 2)
Using C, make 6dc in magic circle. Pull tail to make half-
  moon shape.

TAIL
Using C, [Ch4, miss 1 ch, 1dc in next 2 chs, ss in last] twice.
  Fasten off, leaving a long tail.

FINISHING
Sew two halves of fish together. Sew tail to one end of body
  and flat side of fins to sides of body.

Catnip Mouse

This tiny mouse would be perfect as a gift for a new cat! Fill with a wee sachet of catnip or simply sprinkle some on after finishing – cats will find it completely irresistible.

BODY AND TAIL

Make 6dc in magic circle, pull tail to close.

Rnd 1: *1dc in next dc, 2dc in next dc; rep from * to end. (9 sts)

Rnd 2: *1dc in each of next 2 dc, 2dc in next dc; rep from * to end. (12 sts)

Rnd 3: *1dc in each of next 2 dc, 2dc in next dc; rep from * to end. (16 sts)

Rnd 4: *1dc in each of next 3 dc, 2dc in next dc; rep from * to end. (20 sts)

Rnds 5–7: 1dc in each dc. (20 sts)

Rnd 8: *1dc in each of next 2 dc, dc2tog; rep from * to end. (15 sts)

Rnd 9: *1dc in next dc, dc2tog; rep from * to end. (10 sts)

   Stuff firmly, inserting catnip along with toy stuffing if desired.

Rnd 10: Dc2tog around. (5 sts)

   Insert hook in other side of rem hole and ss to close. Do not cut yarn.

Make tail: Ch10, fasten off.

EARS (MAKE 2)

Make 6dc in magic circle. Pull tail to make half-circle shape.

Row 1: Turn work, ch1, 1dc in each dc across, ss in 1-ch to close.
   Fasten off, leaving long tail for sewing.

FINISHING

Weave in ends. Cut three short lengths of yarn and insert through snout to make whiskers – these will need to be tied firmly or omitted if the toy is being given to a cat.

Sew on ears. Stitch a French knot on either side of face for eyes, using black embroidery thread.

FINISHED SIZES

Mouse: 2cm (¾ in.) long

NOTES

The mouse is made in continuous spiral rounds, so you will not join with a slip stitch. Use a stitch marker throughout to mark the first stitch of each round.

ABBREVIATIONS

ch: chain

dc: double crochet

dc2tog: double crochet 2 together decrease. Insert hook in next st, yrh, pull through a loop. Without finishing st, insert hook in next st, yrh and pull through a loop. Yrh and pull through all three loops on hook

rem: remaining

rep: repeat

Rnd(s): round, rounds

st(s): stitch, stitches

yrh: yarn round hook

MATERIALS

- ¼ x ball, approx 10m (11 yds), of No.8 crochet cotton, such as DMC Perle No.8 100% cotton, in peach
- 1.4mm (US size 9) steel crochet hook
- Toy stuffing
- Small sachet catnip (optional)
- Sewing needle
- Oddment of 6-strand cotton embroidery thread in black

Mama AND Baby Bunny

Mama is teaching Baby how to hop. Sometimes Baby has trouble because his feet are so big... but he's learning, and soon he and Mama will be hopping all over the place together!

MAMA BUNNY

HEAD/BODY

Using A, make 6dc in magic circle, pull tail to close.

Rnd 1: 2dc in each dc. (12 sts)

Rnd 2: *1dc in next dc, 2dc in next dc; rep from * to end. (18 sts)

Rnd 3: *1dc in each of next 2 dc, 2dc in next dc; rep from * to end. (24 sts)

Rnds 4–10: 1dc in each dc.

Rnd 11: *1dc in each of next 2 dc, dc2tog; rep from * to end. (18 sts)

Rnd 12: *1dc in next dc, dc2tog; rep from * to end. (12 sts)
Insert safety eyes and secure. Embroider X for nose in bright pink thread. Stuff firmly.

Rnd 13: Dc2tog around. (6 sts)
Fasten off, leaving a long tail.

ARMS (MAKE 2)

Using A, make 6dc in magic circle, pull tail to close.

Rnd 1: *1dc in next dc, 2dc in next dc; rep from * to end. (9 sts)

Rnds 2–3: 1dc in each dc.
Fasten off, leaving a long tail.

FOOT HALF (MAKE 2 EACH IN A AND B)

Ch5, miss 1 ch, 1dc in each of next 4 chs, turn. (4 sts)

Rows 1–4: Ch1, 1dc in each dc, turn.

Row 5: Ch2, htr4tog.
Fasten off, leaving a long tail.

ABBREVIATIONS

ch(s): chain, chains

dc: double crochet

dc2tog: double crochet 2 together decrease. Insert hook in next st, yrh, pull through a loop. Without finishing st, insert hook in next st, yrh and pull through a loop. Yrh and pull through all three loops on hook

dc3tog: double crochet 3 together decrease. *Insert hook into first st, yrh, pull through a loop. Without finishing st, rep from * into each of next 2 sts. Yrh and pull yarn through all four loops on hook

htr: half treble

htr2tog: half treble 2 together decrease. *Yrh, insert hook into first st, yrh, pull through a loop. Without finishing st, rep from * into next st. Yrh and pull through all five loops on hook

htr3tog: half treble 3 together decrease. *Yrh, insert hook into first st, yrh, pull through a loop. Without finishing st, rep from * into each of next 2 sts. Yrh and pull through all seven loops on hook

htr4tog: half treble 4 together decrease. *Yrh, insert hook into first st, yrh, pull through a loop. Without finishing st, rep from * into each of next 3 sts. Yrh and pull through all nine loops on hook

rep: repeat

Rnd(s): round, rounds

st(s): stitch, stitches

yrh: yarn round hook

MATERIALS

Bunnies

• ½ x 50g ball, approx 60m (65 yds), of 4-ply (baby) yarn, such as Debbie Bliss Baby Cashmerino, in white (A)

• Small amount of 4-ply (fingering) wool, such as King Cole Merino Blend 4-ply 100% wool, in pink (B)

• 2.0mm (US size 4) steel crochet hook

• 2 x pairs of safety eyes

• Toy stuffing

• Oddment of 6-strand embroidery thread in pink

• Sewing needle

Carrots

• 1 skein of 6-strand cotton embroidery thread in orange (A)

• Small amount of 6-strand cotton embroidery thread in green (B)

• 1.5mm (US size 8) steel crochet hook

OUTER EAR (MAKE 2)

Using A, ch6, miss 1 ch, 1dc in each of next 5 chs, turn. (5 sts)

Rows 1–4: Ch1, 1dc in each dc, turn.

Row 5: Ch2, htr2tog, 1htr in next st, htr2tog, turn. (3 sts)

Row 6: Ch1, dc3tog.
  Fasten off, leaving a long tail.

INNER EAR (MAKE 2)

Using B, ch3, miss 1 ch, 1dc in each of next 2 chs, turn. (2 sts)

Rows 1–4: Ch1, 1dc in each dc, turn.

Row 5: Ch2, htr2tog.
  Fasten off, leaving a long tail.

BABY BUNNY

HEAD/BODY

Using A, make 6dc in magic circle, pull tail to close.

Rnd 1: 2dc in each dc. (12 sts)

Rnds 2–7: 1dc in each dc. (12 sts)
  Insert safety eyes and secure. Embroider X for nose in bright pink thread. Stuff firmly.

Rnd 8: Dc2tog around. (6 sts)
  Fasten off, leaving a long tail.

ARMS (MAKE 2)

Using A, make 6dc in magic circle, pull tail to close.

Rnds 1–2: 1dc in each dc. (6 sts)
  Fasten off, leaving a long tail.

FOOT HALF (MAKE 2 EACH IN A AND B)

Ch3, miss 1 ch, 1dc in each of next 2 chs, turn. (2 sts)

Rows 1–2: Ch1, 1dc in each dc, turn.

Row 3: Ch2, htr2tog.
  Fasten off, leaving a long tail.

OUTER EAR (MAKE 2)

Using A, ch4, miss 1 ch, 1dc in each of next 3 chs, turn. (3 sts)

Rows 1–3: Ch1, 1dc in each dc, turn.

Row 4: Ch2, htr3tog.
  Fasten off, leaving a long tail.

INNER EAR (MAKE 2)

Using B, ch2, miss 1 ch, 1dc in next ch, turn. (1 st)

Rows 1–4: Ch1, 1dc in dc, turn.
  Fasten off, leaving a long tail.

Mama Bunny: 6cm (2⅓ in.) tall
Baby Bunny: 4.5cm (1¾ in.) tall
Carrots: 2.5cm (1 in.) long plus 2cm (¾ in.) for tops

FINISHING

Use yarn ends to close hole in each body and to sew arms to bodies.

Sew feet halves in A and B together using whip st and white yarn. Stuff firmly. Sew feet to bodies.

Sew outer ear to inner ear using whip st and white yarn. Stuff firmly. Sew ears to bodies.

CARROT (MAKE 4 OR MORE)

Using A, make 6dc in magic circle; pull tail to close.

Rnds 1–6: 1dc in each dc. (6 sts)

Rnd 7: *1dc in next dc, dc2tog; rep from * to end. (4 sts)
  Fasten off.

FINISHING

Cut three x 5cm (2 in.) lengths of B. Insert hook in top of carrot, fold lengths in half over hook and pull through part way to form loop, then pull all cut ends through loop.

Fuzzy Sheep

It's spring, and the tastiest new growth of green grass has arrived, so Clyde and Nigel, the two black-faced sheep, are munching away all day long. Their coats are long as they haven't been shorn yet, so they are extra fuzzy.

SHEEP
BODY
Work with wrong side facing and loops on outer side of body.
Using A and 2.0mm (US size 4) hook, make 6dc in magic circle. Pull tail to close.

Rnd 1: 2lpdc in each dc. (12 sts)
Rnd 2: *1lpdc in next lpdc, 2lpdc in next lpdc; rep from * to end. (18 sts)
Rnds 3–5: 1lpdc in each lpdc. (18 sts)
Rnd 6: *1lpdc in next lpdc, lpdc2tog; rep from * to end. (12 sts)
Stuff firmly.
Rnds 7–8: lpdc2tog around.
Fasten off, leaving a long tail for sewing.

HEAD
Using B and 1.5mm (US size 8) hook, make 4dc in magic circle. Pull tail to close.

Rnd 1: 2dc in each dc. (8 sts)
Rnd 2: 1dc in each dc. (8 sts)
Rnd 3: 2dc in each dc. (16 sts)

FINISHED SIZES

Sheep: 6cm (2⅓ in.) long, 4cm (1½ in.) tall
Grass patch: 11.5 x 9cm (4½ x 3½ in.)

NOTES
Use one strand of crochet cotton and of laceweight mohair/silk yarn held together throughout.

ABBREVIATIONS
cont: continue
dc: double crochet
dc2tog: double crochet 2 together decrease. Insert hook in next st, yrh, pull through a loop. Without finishing st, insert hook in next st, yrh and pull through a loop. Yrh and pull through all three loops on hook
lpdc: loop double crochet. Insert hook into st, pick up both lengths of yarn looped over tensioning finger (near and far piece), pull both lengths back through st, adjust size of loop, then finish st as usual.
lpdc2tog: loop double crochet 2 together. *Insert hook into first st, pick up both lengths of yarn looped over tension finger and pull both back through st. Without finishing st, rep from * into next st. Yrh and pull through all loops on hook
rep: repeat
Rnd(s): round, rounds
ss: slip stitch
st(s): stitch, stitches
yrh: yarn round hook

MATERIALS
Sheep
• Small amounts of No.5 crochet cotton, such as DMC Petra No.5 100% cotton, and laceweight yarn, such Rowan Kidsilk Haze 70% mohair/30% silk, in white (A)
• Oddment of No.5 crochet cotton such as DMC Petra No.5 100% cotton, in black (B)
• 2.0mm (US size 4) and 1.5mm (US size 8) steel crochet hooks
• Toy stuffing
• Sewing needle
• Scrap of white cotton

Grass patch
• Oddment of No.5 crochet cotton, such as DMC Petra No.5 100% cotton, in green (C)
• 2.0mm (US size 4) steel crochet hook

Rnds 4–7: 1dc in each dc. (16 sts)

Rnd 8: *1dc in each of next 2 dc, dc2tog; rep from * to end. (12 sts)

Rnd 9: Dc2tog around. (6 sts)

Fasten off, leaving a long tail for sewing.

EARS (MAKE 2)

Using B, make 4dc in magic circle. Pull tail to close.

Rnds 1–3: 1dc in each dc.

Fasten off, leaving a long tail for sewing.

LEGS (MAKE 4)

Using B and 1.5mm (US size 8) hook, make 8dc in magic circle. Pull tail to close.

Rnds 1–3: 1dc in each dc. (8 sts)

Ss in next dc.

Fasten off, leaving a long tail for sewing.

FINISHING

Use yarn ends to close holes in body and head. Sew head and legs to body. Attach ears to head.

Using white cotton, embroider eyes on either side of head.

GRASS PATCH FOR SHEEP

Using C and 2.0mm (US size 4) hook, ch31.

Row 1: Miss first ch, 1dc in each ch across, turn. (30 sts)

Row 2: Ch1, lpdc in each dc across, turn.

Row 3: Ch1, 1dc in each st across, turn.

Rep Rows 2 and 3 another 10 times, then work Row 2 again.

Fasten off, weave in ends.

TWO LITTLE *Piggies*

In autumn, Tucker and Wilfred the pigs like to gorge themselves on apples so it's really lucky they live in an apple orchard! Their favourites are the small tart green apples, but they'll take any type they can find.

PIG

HEAD/BODY
Using A, make 8dc in magic circle, pull tail and ss in first st to close.
Rnd 1: Ch1, 1dc in back loop of each dc, ss in first st to close. (8 sts)
Rnd 2: Ch1, *1dc in next dc, 2dc in next dc; rep from * to end, ss in first st to close. (12 sts)
Rnd 3: Rep rnd 2. (18 sts)
Rnds 4–9: Ch1, 1dc in each dc, ss in first st to close. (18 sts)
Rnd 10: Ch1, *1dc in next dc, dc2tog; rep from * to end, ss in first st to close. (12 sts)
Stuff firmly.
Rnd 11: Ch1, dc2tog around, ss in first st to close. (6 sts)
Fasten off, leaving a long tail.

FEET (MAKE 4)
Using A, make 6dc in magic circle, pull tail to close.
Rnd 1: 1dc in back loop of each dc. (6 sts)
Fasten off, leaving a long tail.

EARS (MAKE 2)
Using A, ch4.
Row 1: Miss 1ch, 1dc in each of next 3 chs, turn.
Row 2: 1dc in first st, miss 1 st, 1dc in last st, turn.
Row 3: Dc2tog.
Fasten off, leaving a long tail.

TAIL
Using A, ch5.
Row 1: Miss first ch, 4dc in each of next 4 chs.
Fasten off, leaving a long tail.

MATERIALS
Piggies
- Small amount of No.5 crochet cotton, such as DMC Petra No.5 100% cotton, in pink (A)
- 1.5mm (US size 8) steel crochet hook
- Toy stuffing
- Oddments of 6-strand cotton embroidery thread split into 3 strands, in black and bright pink
- Sewing needle

Apples
- Small amount of No.5 crochet cotton, such as DMC Petra No.5 100% cotton, in green (B)
- 1.5mm (US size 8) steel crochet hook
- Toy stuffing
- Sewing needle

FINISHED SIZES

Piggy: 4cm (1½ in.) long
Apple: about 1cm (½ in.) diameter

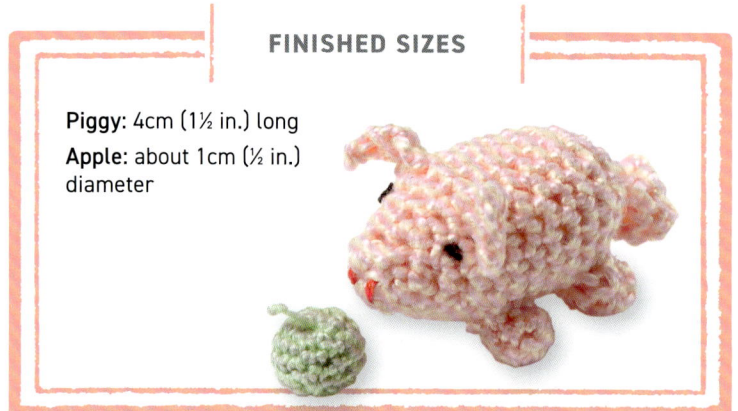

FINISHING
Use yarn ends to close hole in piggie body and to sew on
   feet, ears and tail. Embroider face, using black for eyes
   and bright pink for nostrils.

APPLE
Using B, make 6dc in magic circle, pull tail to close.
Rnd 1: 2dc in each dc. (12 sts)
Rnds 2–4: 1dc in each dc. (12 sts)
   Stuff firmly.
Rnd 5: Dc2tog around. (6 sts)
   Fasten off, leaving a long tail.

FINISHING
Use yarn end to close hole in apple, then draw tail through
   top and bottom of apple several times, pulling tight to form
   dimples. Allow tail to emerge from top of apple, tie knot at
   desired stem length, then cut yarn.

CHAPTER 3

Home Sweet Home

Mini cupcakes and baskets of carrots... all the projects in this chapter are related to the home in some way. A tiny bowl of brightly coloured wrapped sweets is always inviting and the pretty beaded flower pot will certainly brighten up a windowsill or bookshelf. You can even make yourself a plate of sushi!

SENSATIONAL *Sushi*

A tiny maki roll and salmon nigiri sit prettily on their own Japanese-style mini plate. They look good enough to eat!

MAKI
ROLL ENDS (MAKE 2)
Using A, make 6dc in magic circle, pull tail to close.
Rnd 1: 2dc in each dc (12 sts), ss in next st.
  Fasten off A, attach B.
Rnd 2: *1dc in next dc, 2dc in next dc; rep from * to end. (18 sts)
Rnd 3: *1dc in each of next 2 dc, 2dc in next dc; rep from * to end. (24 sts)
Rnd 4: *1dc in each of next 3 dc, 2dc in next dc; rep from * to end. (30 sts)
  Ss in next st, fasten off.

ROLL WRAPPER
Using C, ch32.
Row 1: Miss 2 chs, 1htr in each of next 30 chs, turn. (30 sts)
Row 2: Ch2, 1htr round post of each htr from row below, turn.
Row 3: Ch2, 1htr in each htr across, turn.
Rep Rows 2 and 3 twice more.
  Fasten off.

SALMON NIGIRI
SALMON PIECE SIDE (MAKE 2)
Using A, ch11.
Row 1: Miss 1 ch, 1dc in each of next 10 chs, turn. (10 sts)
Rows 2–15: Ch1, 1dc in each dc across, turn.
  Fasten off.

ABBREVIATIONS
ch(s): chain, chains
dc: double crochet
dc2tog: double crochet 2 together decrease. Insert hook in next st, yrh, pull through a loop. Without finishing st, insert hook in next st, yrh and pull through a loop. Yrh and pull through all three loops on hook
htr: half treble
rep: repeat
Rnd(s): round, rounds
ss: slip stitch
st(s): stitch, stitches
yrh: yarn round hook

MATERIALS
• Small amounts of No.5 crochet cotton, such as DMC Petra No.5 100% cotton, in peach (A), white (B), black (C) and light blue (D)
• 1.5mm (US size 8) steel crochet hook
• Toy stuffing
• Sewing needle

FINISHED SIZES

Sushi: maki roll 3cm (1¼ in.) across, nigiri 5cm (2 in.) long, 2.5cm (1 in.) high
Plate: 7.5cm (3 in.) long, 4cm (1½ in.) wide

RICE

Using B, ch11.

Rnd 1: Miss 1 ch, 3dc in next ch, 1dc in each of next 8 chs, 3dc in last ch. Working down other side of chain, 1dc in each of next 8 chs. (22 sts)

Rnd 2: 2dc in each of next 3 dc, 1dc in each of next 8 dc, 2dc in each of next 3 dc, 1dc in each of next 8 dc. (28 sts)

Rnd 3: [1dc in next dc, 2dc in next dc] 3 times, 1dc in each of next 8 dc, [1dc in next dc, 2dc in next dc] 3 times, 1dc in each of next 8 dc. (34 sts)

Rnd 4: [1dc in each of next 2 dc, 2dc in next dc] 3 times, 1dc in each of next 8 dc, [1dc in each of next 2 dc, 2dc in next dc] 3 times, 1dc in each of next 8 dc. (40 sts)

Rnd 5: [1dc in each of next 3 dc, 2dc in next dc] 3 times, 1dc in each of next 8 dc, [1dc in each of next 3 dc, 2dc in next dc] 3 times, 1dc in each of next 8 dc. (46 sts)

Rnds 6–8: 1dc in each dc. (46 sts)

Rnd 9: [1dc in each of next 3 dc, dc2tog] 3 times, 1dc in each of next 8 dc, [1dc in each of next 3 dc, dc2tog] 3 times, 1dc in each of next 8 dc. (40 sts)

Rnd 10: [1dc in each of next 2 dc, dc2tog] 3 times, 1dc in each of next 8 dc, [1dc in each of next 2 dc, dc2tog] 3 times, 1dc in each of next 8 dc. (34 sts)

Rnd 11: [1dc in next dc, dc2tog] 3 times, 1dc in each of next 8 dc, [1dc in next dc, dc2tog] 3 times, 1dc in each of next 8 dc. (28 sts)

Rnd 12: [Dc2tog] 3 times, 1dc in each of next 8 dc, [dc2tog] 3 times, 1dc in each of next 8 dc. (22 sts)
Stuff firmly.

Rnd 13: Dc2tog around, ss in next dc. (11 sts)
Fasten off, leaving a long tail.

NIGIRI WRAPPER

Using C, ch6.

Row 1: Miss 1 ch, 1dc in each of next 5 chs. (30 sts)

Rows 2–31: Ch1, 1dc in each dc across.
Fasten off, leaving a long tail.

FINISHING

With B, sew maki roll ends to wrapper with whip stitch, stuffing before closing second end.

Sew diagonal lines of back stitch in B on one side of salmon piece side. With A, join two sides with dc join, stuffing lightly before closing last side.

Use yarn end to sew hole in rice closed. Use yarn end to sew nigiri wrapper into a loop. Place around salmon piece and rice.

MINI PLATE

Using D, ch31.

Row 1: Miss 1 ch, 1dc in each of rem 30 chs, turn.

Rows 2–18: Ch1, 1dc in each dc across, turn.
Begin working in rounds for edging.

Rnds 1–2: Ch1, 1dc down sides and into each dc around whole plate, make 1ch at each corner.
Fasten off.

SCRUMPTIOUS *Cake* AND *Tart*

Why not have a tea party with these yummy-looking goodies?
Make the slice of cake in your favourite 'flavours' and the tart
with the 'berries' you love the best.

CAKE SLICE

LAYERS
Using A, ch15.
Row 1: Miss first ch, 1dc in each ch to end, turn.
  (14 sts)
Rows 2–3: Ch1, 1dc in each dc to end, turn.
  Change to B.
Row 4: Ch1, 1dc in each dc to end, turn.
  Change to A.
Rows 5–7: Ch1, 1dc in each dc to end, turn.
  Fasten off.

TOP/BOTTOM (MAKE 2)
Using B and starting with a long tail, ch9.
Row 1: Miss first ch, 1dc in each ch to end, turn. (8 sts)

FINISHED SIZES

Cake slice: 3cm (1¼ in.) tall
Tart: 3.5cm (1⅜ in.) diameter

ABBREVIATIONS

ch(s): chain, chains

dc: double crochet

dc2tog: double crochet 2 together decrease. Insert hook in next st, yrh, pull through a loop. Without finishing st, insert hook in next st, yrh and pull through a loop. Yrh and pull through all three loops on hook

htr: half treble

rep: repeat

Rnd(s): round, rounds

ss: slip stitch

st(s): stitch, stitches

yrh: yarn round hook

MATERIALS

• Small amounts of No.5 crochet cotton, such as DMC Petra No.5 100% cotton, in yellow (A), pink (B), beige (C) and red (D)
• 1.5mm (US size 8) steel crochet hook
• Sewing needle
• Toy stuffing
• Craft/fabric glue (optional)

Row 2: Ch1, dc2tog, 1dc in each of next 4 dc, dc2tog, turn. (6 sts)
Row 3: Ch1, dc2tog, 1dc in each of next 2 dc, dc2tog, turn. (4 sts)
Row 4: Ch1, [dc2tog] twice, turn. (2 sts)
Row 5: Ch1, dc2tog.
  Fasten off, leaving a long tail.

BACK
Using B, ch9.
Row 1: Miss 1ch, 1dc in each ch to end, turn. (8 sts)
Rows 2–7: Ch 1, dc in each dc to end, turn.
  Fasten off.

FINISHING
Use yarn ends to attach top and bottom to layer piece of cake slice using dc. Attach back to cake slice using dc, stuffing before closing the last side.
To make frill at top back of slice, attach yarn in first st, ch2, 2htr in same st, ss in next st, *3htr in next st, ss in next st; rep from * to end.
  Fasten off.

TART
TART BASE
Using C, make 6dc in magic circle, pull tail to close.
Rnd 1: 2dc in each dc. (12 sts)
Rnd 2: *1dc in next dc, 2dc in next dc; rep from * to end. (18 sts)
Rnd 3: *1dc in each of next 2 dc, 2dc in next dc; rep from * to end. (24 sts)
Rnd 4: *1dc in each of next 2 dc, 2dc in next dc; rep from * to end. (32 sts)
Rnd 5: 1dc in back loop of each dc. (32 sts)
Rnd 6: 1dc in each dc. (32 sts)
Rnd 7: Ch2, 4htr in first st, miss 1 st, ss in next st, *miss 1 st, 5htr in next st, miss 1 st, ss in next st; rep from * to end.
  Fasten off.

BERRIES (MAKE 8)
Using D, make 6dc in magic circle, pull tail to close.
Rnds 1–2: 1dc in each dc. (6 sts)
  Fasten off, leaving a long tail.

FINISHING
Stuff each berry firmly. Use yarn end to close hole. Berries can be placed loosely in tart or stitched/glued into place.

Mini Cupcakes ON A PLATE

These teeny cupcakes look just like the real thing. Arrange them on their plate for your next doll tea party or give as tiny favours at your own tea party.

CUPCAKE

BASE

Using A, ch4, join with ss to form ring.

Rnd 1: Ch3, 11tr in ring; ss in top of ch-3 to join.

Rnd 2: Ch1, 1dc in back loop of each tr, join with ss in first dc.

Rnd 3: Ch3, 1tr around post of each dc from rnd below, join with ss in top of first ch-3.

Rnd 4: Ch2, 1tr around post of each tr from rnd below, join with ss in top of first ch-2.
Fasten off.

TOP

Using B, make 6dc in magic circle, pull tail to close.

Rnd 1: 2dc in each dc. (12 sts)

Rnd 2: *1dc in each of next 2 dc, 2dc in next dc; rep from * to end. (16 sts)

Rnd 3: Working in front loops of previous rnd sts only, *5htr in next st, miss 1 st, ss in next st, miss 1 st; rep from * to end, ss in last st to close.
Fasten off, leaving a long tail.

PLATE

Using C, make 6dc in magic circle, pull tail to close.

Rnd 1: 2dc in each dc. (12 sts)

Rnd 2: *1dc in next dc, 2dc in next dc; rep from * to end of round. (18 sts)

Rnd 3: *1dc in each of next 2 dc, 2dc in next dc; rep from * to end. (24 sts)

Rnd 4: *1dc in each of next 3 dc, 2dc in next dc; rep from * to end. (30 sts)

Rnd 5: *1dc in each of next 4 dc, 2dc in next dc; rep from * to end. (36 sts)

Rnd 6: *1dc in each of next 5 dc, 2dc in next dc; rep from * to end. (42 sts)

Rnd 7: *1dc in each of next 6 dc, 2dc in next dc; rep from * to end. (48 sts)

Rnd 8: Ss in next st, *ch3, ss in next st; rep from * to end.
Fasten off.

FINISHING

Using C, embroider cherry in centre of cupcake top. Stuff cake base and then sew top to base with yarn end of top. Weave in ends.

FINISHED SIZES

Cupcake: About 2cm (¾ in.) tall
Plate: 5cm (2 in.) diameter

Flower Box and Pot WITH DOILIES

Sweet little flowers and sparkly beads adorn this tiny box and pot. Use to bring fresh life to a minuscule nook in your home, even in the depths of winter – and make the co-ordinating doilies to finish the look.

BOX

SIDES/BOTTOM (MAKE 5)

Ch7.

Row 1: Miss 1 ch, 1dc in next 6 chs, turn. (6 sts)

Rows 2–6: 1dc in each dc across, turn.
Fasten off.

BASE FOR FLOWERS

Make 6dc in magic circle, pull tail to close.

Rnd 1: 2dc in each dc to end. (12 sts)

Rnd 2: *1dc in next dc, 2dc in next dc; rep from * to end. (18 sts)

Rnd 3: *1dc in each of next 2 dc, 2dc in next dc; rep from * to end. (24 sts)

Rnds 4–6: 1dc in each dc. (24 sts)
Fasten off.

POT

SIDES/BOTTOM

Make 6dc in magic circle, pull tail to close.

Rnd 1: 2dc in each dc to end. (12 sts)

Rnd 2: *1dc in next dc, 2dc in next dc; rep from * to end. (18 sts)

FINISHED SIZES

Flower box: 3cm (1¼ in.) tall, 2.5cm (1 in.) across

Flower pot: 3cm (1¼ in.) tall, 2cm (¾ in.) diameter

Round doily: 4cm (1½ in.) diameter

Star doily: 5.5cm (2³⁄₁₆ in.) from tip to tip

ABBREVIATIONS

ch(s): chain, chains

dc: double crochet

htr: half treble

htr2tog: half treble 2 together decrease. *Yrh, insert hook into first st, yrh, pull through a loop. Without finishing st, rep from * into next st. Yrh, pull yarn through all five loops on hook

rep: repeat

sp: space

ss: slip stitch

st(s): stitch, stitches

tr: treble

tr2tog: treble 2 together decrease. *Yrh, insert hook into first st, yrh, pull through a loop, yrh and pull through first 2 loops on hook. Without finishing st, rep from * into next st. Yrh, pull yarn through all three loops on hook

yrh: yarn round hook

MATERIALS

Box, pot and flower bases

- Small amount of No.5 crochet cotton, such as DMC Petra No.5 100% cotton, in desired colours
- 1.5mm (US size 8) steel crochet hook
- Toy stuffing, if desired
- Sewing needle

Flowers

- Small amount of No.8 crochet cotton, such as DMC Perle No.8 100% cotton, in desired colours
- 1.4mm (US size 9) steel crochet hook
- Glass beads
- Embroidery or sewing thread
- Sewing needle

Doilies

- Small amount of No.8 crochet cotton, such as Rubi Perle No.8 100% cotton, in desired colour
- 1.5mm (US size 8) steel crochet hook

NOTES
To make a striped box as shown, change colour every 2 rows. The flower box shown here has six flowers; there are four in the flower pot.

Rnd 3: 1dc in back loop of each dc. (18 sts)

Rnds 4–8: 1dc in each dc to end. (18 sts)

Rnd 9: With contrasting colour if desired, ch3, 1tr round post of each dc in round below.

Fasten off.

BASE FOR FLOWERS

Make 6dc in magic circle, pull tail to close.

Rnd 1: 2dc in each dc. (12 sts)

Rnds 2–4: 1dc in each dc. (12 sts)

Fasten off.

FLOWERS (MAKE AS MANY AS DESIRED)

Ch4, join with ss to first ch to form a ring.

Rnd 1: Ch1, make 8dc into circle, join with ss to first dc. (8 sts)

Rnd 2: *Ch2, 1htr in same st, 1htr in next st, ch2, ss in same st, ss in next st; rep from * to end. (4 petals made)

Fasten off, leaving a long tail.

FINISHING

Join four side pieces and one bottom piece into box shape using dc.

Use yarn end to sew flowers to flower bases. Use one strand of embroidery thread or machine sewing thread to attach a bead to centre of each flower. Place flower base into box or pot; toy stuffing can be used to fill out each piece if desired.

ROUND DOILY

Ch4, join with ss to first ch to form a ring.

Rnd 1: Ch1, [ch3, 1dc in circle] 5 times, ch3, ss in first ch to join.

Rnd 2: Ch1, 1dc in first ch-3 sp, *ch3, 1dc in next ch-3 sp; rep from * to end, replacing last dc with ss into first dc.

Rnd 3: Ss in next ch-3 sp, ch2, 4htr in same sp, *ch1, 5htr in next ch-3 sp; rep from * to end, ch1, ss in top of first ch-2.

Rnd 4: Ch2, 1htr in next 2 htr, htr2tog, ch3, miss ch-1 sp, *htr2tog, 1htr in next st, htr2tog, ch3, miss ch-1 sp; rep from * to end, ss in top of first htr.

Rnd 5: Ch2, htr2tog, ch3, 1tr in ch3-sp, ch3, *1htr in next htr, htr2tog, ch3, 1tr in ch-3 sp, ch3; rep from * to end, ss in top of first ch-2.

Fasten off.

STAR DOILY

Ch4, join with ss to first ch to form a ring.

Rnd 1: Ch5, [1tr in ring, ch2] 5 times, join with ss in third ch of first ch-5.

Rnd 2: Ss in first ch-2 sp, ch3, 4tr in same sp, ch1, *5tr in next ch-2 sp, ch1; rep from * to end, ss in top of first ch-3.

Note: Rows 3–5 will be worked back and forth in rows on one star point at a time. Cut yarn and rejoin in the next tr group of Round 2 each time, then repeat Rows 3–5 for each point.

Row 3: Ch2, 1tr in next 2 sts, tr2tog, turn.

Row 4: Ch3, tr2tog, turn.

Row 5: Ch2, 1htr in next st.

Fasten off.

Wee Carrots IN A BASKET

Is there anything nicer than fresh, crunchy carrots picked from your own garden? Make this lovely basket heaped high with carrots for a dolls' house garden, or as a gift for your favourite gardener.

CARROT
ROOT (MAKE 4 OR MORE)
Using A, make 6dc in magic circle; pull tail to close.

Rnds 1–6: 1dc in each dc. (6 sts)

Rnd 7: *1dc in next dc, dc2tog; rep from * to end. (4 sts)
Fasten off.

TOP (MAKE ONE FOR EACH ROOT)
Cut three x 5cm (2 in.) lengths of B. Insert hook in top of carrot, fold lengths in half over hook and pull through part way to form loop, then pull cut ends through loop.

BASKET
BASE/SIDES
Using C, ch8.

Rnd 1: Miss 1 ch, 1dc in each of next 6 chs, 3dc in last ch. Working down opposite side of ch, 1dc in each of next 5 chs, 2dc in last ch. (16 sts)

Rnd 2: 2dc in next st, 1dc in each of next 5 sts, 2dc in each of next 3 sts, 1dc in each of next 5 sts, 2dc in each of next 2 sts. (22 sts)

Rnd 3: 2dc in next st, 1dc in each of next 7 sts, 2dc in each of next 4 sts, 1dc in each of next 7 sts, 2dc in each of next 3 sts. (30 sts)

Rnd 4: 2dc in next st, 1dc in each of next 10 sts, [2dc in next st, 1dc in next st] twice, 2dc in next st, 1dc in next 10 sts, [2dc in next st, 1dc in next st] twice. (36 sts)

Rnd 5: 1dc in back loop of each st. (36 sts)

Rnds 6–9: 1dc in each dc. (36 sts)

Rnd 10: Ss in next st, *ch3, miss 1 st, ss in next st; rep from * to end. Fasten off.

ABBREVIATIONS
ch(s): chain, chains
dc: double crochet
dc2tog: double crochet 2 together decrease. Insert hook in next st, yrh, pull through a loop. Without finishing st, insert hook in next st, yrh and pull through a loop. Yrh and pull through all three loops on hook
rep: repeat
Rnd(s): round, rounds
ss: slip stitch
st(s): stitch, stitches
yrh: yarn round hook

MATERIALS
Carrots
- 1 skein of 6-strand cotton embroidery thread in orange (A)
- Small amount of 6-strand cotton embroidery thread in green (B)
- 1.5mm (US size 8) steel crochet hook

Basket
- Small amount of No.5 crochet cotton, such as DMC Petra No.5 100% cotton, in beige (C)
- 1.5mm (US size 8) steel crochet hook
- Sewing needle

FINISHED SIZES

Carrot: 2.5cm (1 in.) long plus 2cm (¾ in.) for tops
Basket: 3cm (1¼ in.) high, 2.5cm (1 in.) wide

NOTES
When using the embroidery thread, use all six strands throughout. One skein of embroidery thread will make about six carrots.

HANDLE
Using C, ch16.

Row 1: Miss 1 ch, 1dc in each dc, turn. (15 sts)

Row 2: *Ch3, miss 1 st, ss in next st; rep from * to end.
  Working down opposite side of ch, rep Row 2.
  Fasten off.

FINISHING
Sew handle to inner rim of basket.

Fresh Fruit BOWL

This is the teeniest tiniest fruit bowl imaginable – it's perfect for a dolls' house or for displaying amongst other small treasures. This project does require some patience, but the result is worth it.

FRUIT
ORANGE
Using A and 1.5mm (US size 8) hook, make 6dc in magic circle. Pull tail to close.

Rnd 1: 2dc in each dc. (12 sts)

Rnd 2: *1dc in next dc, 2dc in next dc; rep from * to end. (18 sts)

Rnds 3–5: 1dc in each dc. (18 sts)

Rnd 6: *1dc in next dc, dc2tog; rep from * to end. (12 sts)
Stuff firmly.

Rnd 7: Dc2tog around. (6 sts)
Cut yarn, leaving a long tail. Thread through rem sts and pull tight to close.

ORANGE LEAF
Using B and 1.5mm (US size 8) hook, ch5, miss first st, 1dc in next st, 1htr in next st, 2tr in next st, ss in last st.
Cut yarn, leaving a long tail for sewing.

APPLE
Using C and 1.5mm (US size 8) hook, make 8dc in magic circle. Pull tail to close.

Rnd 1: 2dc in each dc. (16 sts)

Rnds 2–5: 1dc in each dc. (16 sts)

Rnd 6: *1dc in each of next 2 dc, dc2tog; rep from * to end. (12 sts)

Rnd 7: *1dc in next dc, dc2tog; rep from * to end. (8 sts)
Stuff firmly.

Rnd 8: Dc2tog around. (4 sts)
Cut thread, leaving a long tail. Thread through rem sts and pull tight to close.

FINISHED SIZES

Apple/Orange: about 1cm (½ in.) diameter
Banana: 2.5cm (1 in.) long
Bowl: 3cm (1¼ in.) diameter

ABBREVIATIONS
ch: chain

dc: double crochet

dc2tog: double crochet 2 together decrease. Insert hook in next st, yrh, pull through a loop. Without finishing st, insert hook in next st, yrh and pull through a loop. Yrh and pull through all three loops on hook

htr: half treble

rem: remaining

rep: repeat

Rnd(s): round, rounds

ss: slip stitch

st(s): stitch, stitches

tr: treble

yrh: yarn round hook

MATERIALS
Orange
- Oddments of 6-strand cotton embroidery thread in orange (A)
- Oddment of 6-strand cotton embroidery thread in dark green (B)
- 1.5mm (US size 8) steel crochet hook
- Toy stuffing
- Sewing needle

Apple and banana
- Oddments of No.8 crochet cotton, such as DMC Perle No.8 100% cotton, in pale green (C) and yellow (D)
- Oddment of 6-strand cotton embroidery thread in dark green (B)
- 1.5mm (US size 8) steel crochet hook
- Toy stuffing
- Sewing needle

Fruit bowl
- Oddments of No.8 crochet cotton, such as DMC Perle No.8 100% cotton, in two colours
- 1.75mm (US size 6) steel crochet hook

BANANA

Using C and 1.5mm (US size 8) hook, make 4dc in magic circle, pull tail to close and join with ss in first dc.

Rnds 1–2: Ch1, 1dc in each dc, join with ss in first dc. (4 dc)
Change to D.

Rnd 3: Ch1, *1dc in next dc, 2dc in next dc; rep from * once, join with ss in first dc. (6 sts)

Rnd 4: Ch1, 1dc in each dc, join with ss in first dc. (6 sts)

Rnd 5: Ch1, *1dc in next dc, 2dc in next dc; rep from * twice, join with ss in first dc. (9 sts)

Rnd 6: Ch1, 1dc in each dc, join with ss in first dc. (9 sts)

Rnd 7: Ch1, *1dc in next dc, dc2tog; rep from * twice, join with ss in first dc. (6 sts)

Rnd 8: Ch1, 1dc in each dc, join with ss in first dc. (6 sts)

Rnd 9: Ch1, *1dc in next dc, dc2tog; rep from * once, join with ss in first dc. (4 sts)
Cut yarn, leaving a long tail. Thread through rem sts and pull tight to close.

FINISHING

Sew leaf to top of orange.

For apple, pass length of B through top and bottom of apple several times and pull tight to form dimples. Allow end of thread to emerge from top of apple, tie knot at top of desired length for stem and then cut yarn.

FRUIT BOWL

Change colour each round.

Using 1.75mm (US size 6) hook, make 6dc in magic circle, pull tail to close and join with ss in first dc.

Rnd 1: Ch1, 2dc in each dc, join with ss in first dc. (12 sts)

Rnd 2: Ch1, *1dc in next dc, 2dc in next dc; rep from * to end, join with ss in first dc. (18 sts)

Rnd 3: Ch1, *1dc in each of next 2 dc, 2dc in next dc; rep from * to end, join with ss in first dc. (24 sts)

Rnd 4: Ch1, *1dc in each of next 3 dc, 2dc in next dc; rep from * to end, join with ss in first dc. (30 sts)

Rnd 5: Ch1, *1dc in each of next 4 dc, 2dc in next dc; rep from * to end, join with ss in first dc. (36 sts)

Rnd 6: Ch1, *1dc in each of next 5 dc, 2dc in next dc; rep from * to end, join with ss in first dc. (42 sts)

Rnds 7–9: Ch1, 1dc in each dc, join with ss in first dc. (42 sts)
Cut yarn, weave in ends.

Sweets FOR THE Sweet

These adorable candies look good enough to eat and they can be made in any colour you desire, with stripes or without. Pile several into the pretty candy dish and display – you could also use the small dish as an alternative to hold the fruit on page 69–71, or to keep tiny items of value safe.

SWEETS

MIDDLE SECTION

Using A or B, make 6dc into magic circle, pull tail to close.

Rnd 1: 2dc in each dc. (12 sts)

Rnd 2: *1dc in next dc, 2dc in next dc; rep from * to end. (18 sts)

If making striped sweets, change colour for Rounds 3 and 5.

Rnds 3–6: 1dc in each dc. (18 sts)

Rnd 7: *1dc in next dc, dc2tog; rep from * to end. (12 sts)
   Stuff firmly.

Rnd 8: Dc2tog around. (6 sts)
   Cut yarn, leaving a long tail. Weave through rem sts and pull tight to close.

WRAPPER END (MAKE 2 FOR EACH SWEET)

Using a contrast colour to the sweet if desired and leaving a long tail for sewing on, ch7, 2tr in fourth ch from hook, 1htr in next ch, 1dc in next ch, ss in next ch.

Working down other side of ch, ss in next ch, 1dc in next ch, 1htr in next ch, 2tr in next ch, ch2, ss in same st as last tr.

Cut yarn, weave in last end.

FINISHING

Sew wrapper end to each end of sweets.

FINISHED SIZES

Sweets: 4cm (1½ in.) long

Bowl: 7.5cm (3 in.) diameter

CANDY DISH

Using C, make 6dc into magic circle, pull tail to close.

Rnd 1: 2dc in each dc. (12 sts)

Rnd 2: *1dc in next dc, 2dc in next dc; rep from * around. (18 sts)

Rnd 3: *1dc in each of next 2 dc, 2dc in next dc; rep from * around. (24 sts)

Rnd 4: *1dc in each of next 3 dc, 2dc in next dc; rep from * around. (30 sts)

Rnd 5: *1dc in each of next 4 dc, 2dc in next dc; rep from * around. (36 sts)

Rnd 6: *1dc in each of next 5 dc, 2dc in next dc; rep from * around. (42 sts)

Rnd 7: *1dc in each of next 6 dc, 2dc in next dc; rep from * around. (48 sts)

Rnd 8: *1dc in each of next 7 dc, 2dc in next dc; rep from * around. (54 sts)

Rnds 9–13: 1dc in each dc. (54 sts)

Rnd 14: (Picot edging) *Ss in each of next 2 dc, ch3, ss in same dc as last ss; rep from * to end, ss in first st to end. Cut yarn.

FINISHING

Weave in ends. Pile sweets into bowl.

CHAPTER 4

Pretty Things

We love to adorn our home and ourselves with pretty things, so why not make some? Fashion a tiny bead or flower bracelet for a special person (or yourself!), create a lucky gift with the Four Leaf Clover Keychain or decorate a treasured spot with the Russian Doll Sisters. There are also great ideas for the festive season, such as the Snowman and Bauble Cover, which can be displayed for maximum sweet effect with the Itty-bitty Snowflake Garland.

Russian Doll SISTERS

Ekaterina, Elena and Eva are three sisters who live in the highest onion dome of a very ancient building in St Petersburg, Russia. They like to eat blini with fresh strawberries and embroider themselves new dresses.

FINISHED SIZES

Eva: 4cm (1½ in.) tall
Elena: 4.5cm (1¾ in.) tall
Ekaterina: 5cm (2 in.) tall

ABBREVIATIONS

beg: beginning
dc: double crochet
dc2tog: double crochet 2 together decrease. Insert hook in next st, yrh, pull through a loop. Without finishing st, insert hook in next st, yrh and pull through a loop. Yrh and pull through all three loops on hook
dtr: double treble
htr: half treble
st(s): stitch, stitches
tr: treble
rem: remaining
rep: repeat
Rnd(s): round, rounds
yrh: yarn round hook

MATERIALS

Eva (smallest Russian doll)
• ¼ x ball, approx 10m (11 yds), of No.8 crochet cotton, such as DMC Perle No.8 100% cotton, in peach (MC)
• ¼ x ball, approx 10m (11 yds), of No.8 crochet cotton, such as DMC Perle No.8 100% cotton, in turquoise (CC)
• 1.4mm (US size 9) steel crochet hook

Elena (middle Russian doll)
• ⅛ x ball, approx 25m (27 yds), of No.5 crochet cotton, such as DMC Petra Perle No.5 100% cotton, in pale blue (MC)
• ⅛ x ball, approx 25m (27 yds), of No.5 crochet cotton, such as DMC Petra Perle No.5 100% cotton, in lilac (CC)
• 1.75mm (US size 6) steel crochet hook

Ekaterina (biggest Russian doll)
• ⅛ x ball, approx 34m (37 yds), of 4-ply (fingering) cotton yarn, such as Rowan Summerlite 4-ply 100% cotton, in pink (MC)
• ⅛ x ball, approx 34m (37 yds), of 4-ply (fingering) cotton yarn, such as Rowan Summerlite 4-ply 100% cotton, in green (CC)
• 2.0mm (US size 4) steel crochet hook

All dolls
• Toy stuffing
• Sewing needle
• Cream felt for face and dress panel
• Yellow felt for hair
• Oddments of embroidery thread in green, pink and blue
• Powder blush for cheeks
• Craft/fabric glue

EVA

Using MC and 1.4mm (US size 9) hook, make 6dc in magic circle.

Rnd 1: 2dc in each dc. (12 sts)

Rnd 2: *1dc in next dc, 2dc in next dc; rep from * to end. (18 sts)

Rnd 3: *1dc in each of next 2 dc, 2dc in next dc; rep from * to end. (24 sts)

Rnds 4–7: 1dc in each dc. (24 sts)

Rnd 8: 1dc in back loop of each dc. (24 sts)
Change to CC.

Rnd 9: *1dc in each of next 3 dc, 2dc in next dc; rep from * to end. (30 sts)

Rnds 10–11: 1dc in each dc. (30 sts)

Rnd 12: *1dc in each of next 4 dc, 2dc in next dc; rep from * to end. (36 sts)

Rnds 13–14: 1dc in each dc. (36 sts)

Rnd 15: *1dc in each of next 4 dc, dc2tog; rep from * to end. (30 sts)

Rnd 16: *1dc in each of next 3 dc, dc2tog; rep from * to end. (24 sts)

Rnd 17: *1dc in each of next 2 dc, dc2tog; rep from * to end. (18 sts)

Rnd 18: *1dc in next dc, dc2tog; rep from * to end. (12 sts)
Stuff firmly.

Rnd 19: Dc2tog around. (6 sts)
Cut yarn, leaving a long tail. Thread through rem sts and pull tight to close.

ELENA

Using MC and 1.75mm (US size 6) hook, make 6dc in magic circle.

Rnd 1: 2dc in each dc. (12 sts)

Rnd 2: *1dc in next dc, 2dc in next dc; rep from * to end. (18 sts)

Rnd 3: *1dc in each of next 2 dc, 2dc in next dc; rep from * to end. (24 sts)

Rnds 4–7: 1dc in each dc. (24 sts)

Rnd 8: 1dc in back loop of each dc. (24 sts)
Change to CC.

Rnd 9: *1dc in each of next 3 dc, 2dc in next dc; rep from * to end. (30 sts)

Rnds 10–14: 1dc in each dc. (30 sts)

Rnd 15: *1dc in each of next 3 dc, dc2tog; rep from * to end. (24 sts)

Rnd 16: *1dc in each of next 2 dc, dc2tog; rep from * to end. (18 sts)

Rnd 17: *1dc in next dc, dc2tog; rep from * to end. (12 sts)
Stuff firmly.

Rnd 18: Dc2tog around. (6 sts)
Cut yarn, leaving a long tail. Thread through rem sts and pull tight to close.

EKATERINA

Using MC and 2.0mm (US size 4) hook, make 6dc in magic circle.

Rnd 1: 2dc in each dc. (12 sts)

Rnd 2: *1dc in next dc, 2dc in next dc; rep from * to end. (18 sts)

Rnd 3: *1dc in each of next 2 dc, 2dc in next dc; rep from * to end. (24 sts)

Rnds 4–8: 1dc in each dc. (24 sts)

Rnd 9: 1dc in back loop of each dc. (24 sts)
Change to CC.

Rnd 10: *1dc in each of next 3 dc, 2dc in next dc; rep from * to end. (30 sts)

Rnds 11–12: 1dc in each dc. (30 sts)

Rnd 13: *1dc in each of next 4 dc, 2dc in next dc; rep from * to end. (36 sts)

Rnds 14–15: 1dc in each dc. (36 sts)

Rnd 16: *1dc in each of next 4 dc, dc2tog; rep from * to end. (30 sts)

Rnd 17: *1dc in each of next 3 dc, dc2tog; rep from * to end. (24 sts)

Rnd 18: *1dc in each of next 2 dc, dc2tog; rep from * to end. (18 sts)

Rnd 19: *1dc in next dc, dc2tog; rep from * to end. (12 sts)
Stuff firmly.

Rnd 20: Dc2tog around. (6 sts)
Cut yarn, leaving a long tail. Thread through rem sts and pull tight to close.

NOTES
All three dolls are made in continuous spiral rounds, so you will not join with a slip stitch. Use a stitch marker throughout to mark the first stitch of each round.

SHAWL (ALL DOLLS)

Using MC, holding piece upside down and working into front loops, start
in 13th st from the beg of Round 8 (Round 9 for Ekaterina), 2dc in next
st, 2htr in each of next 2 sts, 2tr in each of next 2 sts, 2dtr in each of
next 14 sts, 2tr in each of next 2 sts, 2htr in each of next 2 sts, 2dc in
next st.
Fasten off.

FINISHING

Cut short length of MC and tie through two front dc of shawl to make
a bow.
Cut circle from cream felt for face. Cut hair shape from yellow felt and
glue to top of face with craft glue. Using blue embroidery thread,
embroider French knots for eyes. Using pink embroidery thread, work
back stitch for mouth. Using a cotton swab, apply powder blush to
cheeks in small circles. Glue face to front of head.
Cut dress panel shape from cream felt. Embroider flowers in lazy daisy
stitch using blue, green and pink embroidery thread and work back
stitch in green for the vines. Glue dress panel to front of dress, fitting
under front of shawl.

TINY *Flowers Bracelet*

This simple pattern can be customised to suit your style with different colours or flower placement, or even by adding beading or sequins. It's perfect for spring, or when you just want to feel springlike!

FLOWER (MAKE 8)
Using A, ch4, join with ss to form a ring.
Rnd 1: Ch1, make 10dc in ring, ss in first dc to close.
Rnd 2: *Ch2, 1htr in same st, 1htr in next st, ch2, ss in same st, ss in next st; rep from * to end.
  Fasten off, leaving a long tail for sewing.

BRACELET BAND
Using B, ch51.
Row 1: 1dc in second ch from hook and each ch across, turn. (50 sts)
Rows 2–5: Ch1, 1dc in each dc across, turn.
At the end of Row 5, ss across short end of band to centre, ch6, then ss in same place as last ss to form button loop.
  Fasten off.

FINISHING
Weave in all ends except one long end on each flower for sewing.
Sew button to non-loop end of bracelet band. Sew flowers to band in desired placement.

ABBREVIATIONS
ch(s): chain, chains
dc: double crochet
htr: half treble
rep: repeat
Rnd: round
ss: slip stitch
st(s): stitch, stitches

MATERIALS
- Small amounts of No.5 crochet cotton, such as DMC Petra No.5 100% cotton, in various colours (A)
- Oddment of No.5 crochet cotton, such as DMC Petra No.5 100% cotton, in green (B)
- 1.5mm (US size 8) steel crochet hook
- Sewing needle
- 1 x 1cm (½ in.) diameter button

FINISHED SIZES
Flower: 2cm (¾ in.) diameter
Bracelet: 17.5cm (6⅞ in.) long

ITTY BITTY *Snowflake Garland*

Let it snow, let it snow, let it snow! During the festive season, this pretty garland is the perfect touch for bookshelves, doorways, or even a spot on the tree. Make it as long as you like by adding more snowflakes. It crochets up quickly and easily, and the fuzzy mohair makes a beautiful halo around each flake.

ABBREVIATIONS
ch(s): chain, chains
dc: double crochet
htr: half treble
rep: repeat
Rnd: round
sp: space
ss: slip stitch

MATERIALS
- ¼ x ball, approx 52m (57 yds), of laceweight yarn, such Rowan Kidsilk Haze 70% mohair/30% silk, in white
- 1.5mm (US size 8) steel crochet hook

NOTES
One 25g ball of laceweight yarn will be enough to make a sizable garland – the sample shown used less than ¼ of a ball. You could add more chains between each of the snowflakes if you prefer to have a longer garland.

SNOWFLAKES
Ch4, join with ss to form a ring.
Rnd 1: *Ch5, [1htr in ring, ch3] 6 times, join with ss in second ch of first ch-5.
Rnd 2: [2dc, ch4, 2dc] in each ch-3 sp, join with ss in first dc.
Ch14, join with ss in fourth ch from hook to form ring for next snowflake; rep from * until garland is desired length.

FINISHING
Weave in ends.

FINISHED SIZES

Each snowflake: 3cm (1¼ in.) diameter

Snowman AND Bauble Cover

Decorative delights for the festive season – Mr Snowman can also easily be transformed into an ornament by running a loop of ribbon through his head. The bauble cover was made for a 6.5cm (2½ in.) diameter bauble, but could be made for any size bauble by increasing in any round.

SNOWMAN

BODY

Using A and 2.0mm (US size 4) hook, make 6dc in magic circle, pull tail to close.

Rnd 1: 2dc in each dc. (12 sts)

Rnd 2: 2dc in each dc. (24 sts)

Rnd 3: *1dc in next dc, 2dc in next dc; rep from * to end. (36 sts)

Rnds 4–13: 1dc in each dc. (36 sts)

Rnd 14: *1dc in each of next 4 dc, dc2tog; rep from * to end. (30 sts)

Rnd 15: *1dc in each of next 3 dc, dc2tog; rep from * to end. (24 sts)

Rnd 16: *1dc in each of next 2 dc, dc2tog; rep from * to end. (18 sts)

Fasten off.

HEAD

Using A and 2.0mm (US size 4) hook, make 6dc in magic circle, pull tail to close.

Rnd 1: 2dc in each dc. (12 sts)

Rnd 2: *1dc in next dc, 2dc in next dc; rep from * to end. (18 sts)

Rnd 3: *1dc in each of next 2 dc, 2dc in next dc; rep from * to end. (24 sts)

Rnd 4: *1dc in each of next 3 dc, 2dc in next dc; rep from * to end. (30 sts)

Rnds 5–8: 1dc in each dc. (30 sts)

Rnd 9: *1dc in each of next 3 dc, dc2tog; rep from * to end. (24 sts)

Rnd 10: *1dc in each of next 2 dc, dc2tog; rep from * to end. (18 sts)

Fasten off, leaving a long tail.

ABBREVIATIONS

cont: continue

ch(s): chain, chains

dc: double crochet

dc2tog: double crochet 2 together decrease. Insert hook in next st, yrh, pull through a loop. Without finishing st, insert hook in next st, yrh and pull through a loop. Yrh and pull through all three loops on hook

dtr2tog: double treble 2 together decrease. *Yrh twice, insert hook into first st, yrh, pull through a loop, [yrh and pull through two loops on hook] twice. Without finishing st, rep from * into next st. Yrh and pull yarn through all three loops on hook

rep: repeat

Rnd(s): round, rounds

sp: space

ss: slip stitch

st(s): stitch, stitches

tr: treble

tr2tog: treble 2 together decrease. *Yrh, insert hook into first st, yrh, pull through a loop, yrh and pull yarn through first two loops on hook. Without finishing st, rep from * into next st. Yrh and pull yarn through all three loops on hook

yrh: yarn round hook

MATERIALS

Snowman

- ½ x ball, approx 44m (48 yds), of 4-ply (baby) yarn, such as Debbie Bliss Baby Cashmerino 50% cashmere/50% merino, in white (A)
- 2.0mm (US size 4) steel crochet hook
- 5 x 6mm (¼ in.) safety eyes
- Toy stuffing
- Sewing needle

Hat and scarf

- Small amount of DK (light worsted) weight cotton yarn in black (B)

- Small amount of DK (light worsted) weight wool in red (C)
- 2.5mm (US size 2) steel crochet hook
- Sewing needle

Carrot nose

- Small amount of 6-strand cotton embroidery thread divided into 3 strands, in orange (D)
- 1.5mm (US size 8) steel crochet hook
- Sewing needle

Bauble cover

- Small amount of No.5 crochet cotton, such as DMC Petra No.5 100% cotton, in white (E)
- 1.5mm (US size 8) steel crochet hook

HAT

Using B and 2.5mm (US size 2) hook, make 6dc in magic circle, pull tail to close.

Rnd 1: 2dc in each dc. (12 sts)

Rnd 2: *1dc in next dc, 2dc in next dc; rep from * to end. (18 sts)

Rnd 3: 1dc in back loop of each dc.

Rnds 4–7: 1dc in each dc.

Rnd 8: 2dc in front loop of each dc. (36 sts)
Fasten off.

SCARF

Using C and 2.5mm (US size 2) hook, ch41, miss 1 ch, ss in next ch, 1dc in each ch to last ch, ss in last ch. Fasten off.

SCARF END BALLS (MAKE 2)

Using C and 2.5mm (US size 2) hook, make 6dc in magic circle, pull tail to close.

Rnd 1: 1dc in each dc. (6 sts)
Fasten off, leaving a long tail.

CARROT NOSE

Using D and 1.5mm (US size 8) hook, make 4dc in magic circle, pull tail to close.

Rnds 1–2: 1dc in each dc.
Fasten off, leaving a long tail.

FINISHING

Insert safety eyes in snowman head and secure. Insert safety eyes as buttons down the front of body. Stuff head and body firmly. Sew head to body. Sew nose to head.

Push each end of scarf into a scarf end ball and sew in place.

BAUBLE COVER

Using E and 1.5mm (US size 8) hook, ch4, join with a ss in first ch to form a ring.

Rnd 1: Ch5, [1tr in ring, ch2] 5 times, join with a ss in third of first ch-5.

Rnd 2: Ss in first ch-2 sp, ch3, 2tr in same sp, *ch2, 3tr in next sp; rep from * to end, ch2, join with a ss in top of first ch-3.

Rnd 3: Ch4, miss 1 tr, 1dtr in next tr, *ch3, 1tr in ch 2 sp, ch3, dtr2tog in first and third tr; rep from * to end, ch3, 1tr in ch-2 sp, ch3, join with a ss in top of first tr.

Rnd 4: Ch3, *4tr in next ch-3 sp, ch1; rep from * to end, ss in top of first ch-3.

Rnd 5: Ss in next st, ch2, 1tr in next st, tr2tog in next 2 tr, *ch2, [tr2tog in next 2 tr] twice; rep from * to end, ch2, join with a ss in top of first tr.

Insert bauble after this round and cont crocheting around bauble.

Rnd 6: Ch2, 1tr in tr2tog, ch3, *tr2tog in next two tr2tog, ch3; rep from * to end, join with a ss in top of first tr.

Rnd 7: Ch1, *ch3, 1dc in top of tr2tog; rep from * to end, join with a ss in top of first ch.

Rnd 8: Ss in next ch-3 sp, *ch1, [1dc, ch3, 1dc] all in same sp; rep in each sp from * to end, ch1, join with a ss in first dc.
Fasten off.

Snowman: 6.5cm (2½ in.) tall
Bauble cover: 6.5cm (2½ in.) diameter

Easter Eggs AND Baby Chick

Tufty the chick is waiting for his brother and sisters to hatch. He keeps asking his mum, Henny Pen, when they'll come out of their colourful shells. In the meantime, he likes to spend lots of time with the eggs, talking to them and playing them music.

EGG (SEE NOTES OPPOSITE)

Using A, make 6dc in magic circle.

Rnd 1: 2dc in each dc. (12 sts)

Rnd 2: *1dc in next dc, 2dc in next dc; rep from * to end. (18 sts)

Rnds 3–7: 1dc in each dc. (18 sts)

Rnd 8: *1dc in next dc, dc2tog; rep from * to end. (12 sts)

Rnds 9–10: 1dc in each dc. (12 sts)

Stuff firmly.

Rnd 11: *1dc in next dc, dc2tog; rep from * to end. (8 sts)

Fasten off, leaving a long tail.

CHICK

BODY

Follow egg pattern, using B. Insert safety eyes and secure after Round 10.

WINGS (MAKE 2)

Using B, make 6dc in magic circle.

Pull tail to make half-moon shape.

Fasten off, leaving a long tail.

FEET

Using orange, [ch4, miss first ch, 1dc in next 3 chs, ss in same ch as last dc] twice.

Fasten off, leaving a long tail.

FINISHED SIZES

Egg: 3.5cm (1⅜ in.) tall

Chick: 4cm (1½ in.) tall

FINISHING

Close hole in top of eggs and chick body using yarn end. Sew wings and feet to chick body.

Cut small triangle of orange felt and stick to chick face to form beak.

Cut short lengths of B and pull through top of chick head, then unravel to form a tuft.

ABBREVIATIONS

ch(s): chain, chains

dc: double crochet

dc2tog: double crochet 2 together decrease. Insert hook in next st, yrh, pull through a loop. Without finishing st, insert hook in next st, yrh and pull through a loop. Yrh and pull through all three loops on hook

rep: repeat

Rnd(s): round, rounds

ss: slip stitch

st(s): stitch, stitches

yrh: yarn round hook

MATERIALS

Eggs

- Small amounts of 4-ply (baby) yarn, such as King Cole Merino Blend 4-ply 100% wool, in pink, blue and white (A)
- 2.0mm (US size 4) steel crochet hook
- Toy stuffing
- Sewing needle

Chick

- Small amount of 4-ply (baby) yarn, such as King Cole Merino Blend 4-ply 100% wool, in yellow (B)
- 2.0mm (US size 4) steel crochet hook
- 1 x pair 6mm (¼ in.) safety eyes
- Toy stuffing
- Small amount of DK (light worsted) cotton, such as Knit Picks CotLin 70% cotton/30% linen, in orange
- Sewing needle
- Small piece of orange felt
- Craft/fabric glue

NOTES
For the striped egg, alternate colours every two rounds. For the half-and-half egg, change colour after round 5. For the 3-band egg, change colour after round 2 and again after round 7.

TINY *Bead Bracelet*

This pretty bracelet can be made in pastels, as shown, for a soft look, or bright colours for more of a kick. The bracelet shown is made with nine beads, but you can make as many as desired for a longer or shorter length. You could even make a matching necklace by making more beads and threading them in the same way.

BEADS (MAKE 2 IN EACH COLOUR)

Make 6dc in magic circle, pull tail to close.
Rnd 1: 2dc in each dc. (12 sts)
Rnds 2–4: 1dc in each dc. (12 sts)
   Stuff firmly.
Rnd 5: Dc2tog around. (6 sts)
   Cut yarn, leaving a long tail. Thread through rem sts and pull tight to close.

FINISHING

String beads onto a length of crochet cotton, tying a knot between each (use sewing needle to keep knot close to bead while tightening). Tie into a bow, or attach two halves of a jewellery clasp if desired.

ABBREVIATIONS

dc: double crochet
dc2tog: double crochet 2 together decrease. Insert hook in next st, yrh, pull through a loop. Without finishing st, insert hook in next st, yrh and pull through a loop. Yrh and pull through all three loops on hook
rem: remaining
Rnd(s): round, rounds
st(s): stitch, stitches
yrh: yarn round hook

MATERIALS

- Oddments of No.5 crochet cotton, such as DMC Petra No.5 100% cotton, in three colours
- 1.5mm (US size 8) steel crochet hook
- Toy stuffing
- Sewing needle
- Jewellery clasp (optional)

FINISHED SIZES

Bead: 1.2cm (½ in.) diameter
Bracelet: 15cm (6 in.) (excluding ties)

NOTES

The beads are made in continuous spirals, so you will not join with a slip stitch. Use a stitch marker throughout to mark the first stitch of each round.

Four-leaf Clover KEYCHAIN

Bring the luck of the Irish to all your friends – this clever four-leaf clover is quick and easy to make, making it the perfect last-minute gift for any friend who loses keys.

CLOVER LEAVES (MAKE 8 HALVES)

Row 1: Ch3, miss 1 ch, 1dc in each of next 2 chs, turn. (2 sts)
Row 2: Ch1, 1dc in each dc, turn.
Row 3: Ch1, 2dc in each of next 2 dc, turn. (4 sts)
Row 4: Ch1, 1dc in each dc, turn.
Row 5: Ch1, 2dc in next dc, 1dc in each of next 2 dc, 2dc in last dc, turn. (6 sts)
Row 6: Ch1, 1dc in each dc, turn.
Row 7: Ch1, [1dc, 1htr] in next dc, [1tr, 1htr] in next dc, ss in next dc, [1htr, 1tr] in next dc, [1htr, 1dc] in next dc, ss in last dc.
Fasten off, leaving a long tail.

STEM

Ch11, miss 1 ch, 1dc in next 10 dc.
Fasten off, leaving a long tail.

FINISHING

Use yarn end to sew two halves of a leaf together with whip stitch, stuffing lightly before closing final side. Rep for rem three leaves.
Sew base of all four leaves together in clover shape.
Sew stem to clover, then sew keychain finding to back of clover.
Sew button to middle of clover, if desired.

FINISHED SIZES

Clover: 4cm (1½ in.) across

SWEET *Gingerbread Cottage*

Can you imagine who lives inside this tiny cottage? Perhaps it's a family of ladybirds, or honeybees. Whoever it is, they like to keep things looking neat as a pin, with lots of colourful roof tiles and well-maintained topiary bushes in the front garden.

COTTAGE

FRONT AND BACK (MAKE 2)
Using A, ch11.
Row 1: Miss first ch, 1dc in each ch to end, turn. (10 sts)
Rows 2–10: Ch1, 1dc in each dc to end, turn.
Rows 11–13: Ch1, dc2tog, 1dc in each dc to last 2 sts, dc2tog, turn.
Row 14: Ch1, [dc2tog] twice, turn.
Row 15: Ch1, dc2tog.
  Fasten off.

SIDES AND BASE (MAKE 3)
Using A, ch11.
Row 1: Miss first ch, 1dc in each ch to end, turn. (10 sts)
Rows 2–10: Ch1, 1dc in each dc to end, turn.
  Fasten off.

ROOF (MAKE 2)
Using B, ch11.
Row 1: Miss first ch, 1dc in each ch to end, turn. (10 sts)
Rows 2–9: Ch1, 1dc in each dc to end, turn.
Row 10: Ch3, 2tr in same st, miss 1 st, ss in next st, miss 1 st, 5tr in next st, miss 1 st, ss in next st, miss 1 st, 3tr in last st.
  Fasten off.

ABBREVIATIONS
ch(s): chain, chains
dc: double crochet
dc2tog: double crochet 2 together decrease. Insert hook in next st, yrh, pull through a loop. Without finishing st, insert hook in next st, yrh and pull through a loop. Yrh and pull through all three loops on hook
htr: half treble
rep: repeat
Rnd(s): round, rounds
ss: slip stitch
st(s): stitch, stitches
tr: treble
yrh: yarn round hook

MATERIALS
- Small amount of No.5 crochet cotton, such as DMC Petra No.5 100% cotton, in pink (A)
- Oddments of No.5 crochet cotton, such as DMC Petra No.5 100% cotton, in white (B) green (C), yellow (D), blue (E) and peach (F)
- 1.5mm (US size 8) steel crochet hook
- Toy stuffing
- Oddments of 6-strand cotton embroidery thread in grey and pink
- Sewing needle

FINISHED SIZES

Cottage: 4.5cm (1¾ in.) tall, 5cm (2 in.) across eave to eave
Topiary bushes: 2.5cm (1 in.) tall

ROOF TILES (MAKE 2 IN EACH COLOUR)
Using C, D, E or F, ch11.
Row 1: Miss 2 chs, 2htr in next ch, miss 1 ch, ss in next ch, miss 1 ch, 5htr in next ch, miss 1 ch, ss in next ch, miss 1 ch, 3htr in last ch.
Fasten off, leaving a long tail for sewing.

WINDOWS (MAKE 2)
Using B, ch3.
Row 1: Miss first ch, 1dc in next 2 chs, turn. (2 sts)
Row 2: Ch1, 1dc in each of next 2 dc.
Fasten off, leaving a long tail for sewing.

DOOR
Using B, ch4.
Row 1: Miss first ch, 1dc in each of next 3 chs, turn. (3 sts)
Rows 2-4: Ch1, 1dc in each dc across, turn.
Fasten off, leaving a long tail for sewing.

FINISHING
Join all the cottage wall pieces together with dc. Stuff cottage firmly and attach roof with dc. Sew tiles to roof, overlapping each layer slightly.
Use grey embroidery thread to stitch window detail. Sew windows to front of cottage.
Make a French knot in pink embroidery thread for doorknob. Sew door to front of cottage.

TOPIARY BUSHES (MAKE 2, OR MORE)
POT
Using F, ch2.
Rnd 1: 6dc in 2nd ch from hook.
Rnd 2: 2dc in each dc. (12 sts)
Rnd 3: 1dc in back loop of each dc. (12 sts)
Rnds 4-5: 1dc in each dc, ss in last dc to close. (12 sts)
Rnd 6: Ch2, 1htr in each dc, ss to close.
Fasten off.

BUSH
Using C, make 6dc in magic circle. Pull tail to close.
Rnd 1: 2dc in each dc. (12 sts)
Rnd 2: *1dc in next dc, 2dc in next dc; rep from * to end. (18 sts)
Rnds 3-5: 1dc in each dc. (10 sts)
Rnd 6: *1dc in next dc, dc2tog; rep from * to end. (12 sts)
Stuff firmly.
Rnd 7: Dc2tog around. (6 sts)
Fasten off, leaving a long tail.

FINISHING
Use tail to close hole in bush, stitch bush to top of pot.

CHAPTER 5

Tiny Friends

Who can resist smiling Dante the Dolphin, Annabelle the Doll with her own removable dress or teeny weeny spotted ladybirds complete with a leaf to sit on? You will love to make stripey Stanley the Snail – easily created with self-striping yarn – or beautiful colourful fish in their own fishing net. Use fine artistic wire to curve Clive the Fuzzy Caterpillar into a distinctive shape, and don't forget the leaf accessories!

Tropical Fish AND Starfish WITH Net

Colourfully striped tropical fish and a bright starfish are suspended in their own 'fishing net', a neat drawstring bag that can be used in many other ways.

TROPICAL FISH
HEAD/BODY
Using first colour and 1.0mm (US size 12) hook, make 6dc in magic circle. Pull tail to close.

Rnd 1: 2dc in each dc. (12 sts)
Rnd 2: *1dc in next dc, 2dc in next dc; rep from * to end. (18 sts)
Rnds 3–7: 1dc in each dc. (18 sts)
  Change to second colour.
Rnds 8–9: 1dc in each dc. (18 sts)
  Change to first colour.
Rnds 10–11: 1dc in each dc. (18 sts)
  Change to second colour.
Rnds 12–13: 1dc in each dc. (18 sts)
  Change to first colour.
Rnd 14: *1dc in next dc, dc2tog; rep from * to end. (12 sts)
Rnd 15: 1dc in each dc. (12 sts)
  Stuff lightly.
Rnd 16: Dc2tog around. (6 sts)
  Fasten off.

TAIL (MAKE 2)
Using second colour and 1.0mm (US size 12) hook, make 6dc in magic circle, pull tail to close.

FINISHED SIZES

Fish: 4cm (1½ in.) long
Starfish: 4.5cm (1¾ in.) across

Rnd 1: 2dc in each dc. (12 sts)

Rnd 2: 1dc in each dc. (12 sts)

Rnd 3: Dc2tog to 3 sts.

Fasten off, leaving a long tail.

EYE WHITES (MAKE 2)

Using A and 1.5mm (US size 8) hook, make 8dc in magic circle, pull tail to close.

Fasten off, leaving a long tail.

STARFISH (MAKE 2)

Using B and 1.0mm (US size 12) hook, make 6dc in magic circle, pull tail to close.

Rnd 1: 2dc in each dc. (12 sts)

Rnd 2: *1dc in next dc, 2dc in next dc; rep from * to end. (18 sts)

Rnd 3: *1dc in each of next 2 dc, 2dc in next dc; rep from * to end. (24 sts)

Rnd 4: *1dc in each of next 3 dc, 2dc in next dc; rep from * to end. (30 sts)

Row 1 of arm: Without cutting yarn, ch1, 1dc in each of next 6 dc, turn.

Row 2: Ch1, 1dc in each of 6 dc, turn. (6 sts)

Row 3: Ch1, dc2tog, 1dc in each of next 2 dc, dc2tog, turn. (4 sts)

Row 4: Ch1, 1dc in each of next 4 dc, turn.

Row 5: Ch1, [dc2tog] twice, turn. (2 sts)

Row 6: Ch1, 1dc in each of next 2 dc, turn.

Row 7: Ch1, dc2tog.

Fasten off.

Reattach yarn to work Rows 1–7 of arm on next 6 sts of rnd 4. Rep on foll 6 sts each time until all 5 arms are complete.

NET BAG

Using E and 2.5mm (US size 2) hook, ch4, join with ss to first ch to form a ring.

Rnd 1: 12dc into ring.

Rnd 2: *1dc in next dc, 2dc in next dc; rep from * to end. (18 sts)

Rnd 3: *1dc in each of next 2 dc, 2dc in next dc; rep from * to end. (24 sts)

Rnd 4: *1dc in each of next 3 dc, 2dc in next dc; rep from * to end. (30 sts)

Rnd 5: *1dc in each of next 4 dc, 2dc in next dc; rep from * to end. (36 sts)

Rnd 6: *1dc in each of next 5 dc, 2dc in next dc; rep from * to end. (42 sts)

Rnd 7: Ss in next dc, *ch6, miss 2 dc, 1dc in next dc; rep from * to end, ss in first 6-ch sp to join.

Rnds 8–15: *Ch6, 1dc in next ch-6 sp; rep from * ending ch6, miss 2 sts, 1dc in first ch-6 sp.

Ch60, fasten off.

FINISHING

Sew both halves of fish tail to end of body.

Use black embroidery thread to embroider inner eye on eye whites. Sew eyes to fish.

Join two halves of starfish together with dc, stuffing lightly before joining second edge of final arm.

Weave length of ch through top of net and pull closed as a drawstring.

Dante the Dolphin

Splish splash! Dante the playful dolphin loves to frolic in the sea with his friends. He's always happy, as his smiling face shows.

ABBREVIATIONS

ch(s): chain, chains

dc: double crochet

dc2tog: double crochet 2 together decrease. Insert hook in next st, yrh, pull through a loop. Without finishing st, insert hook in next st, yrh and pull through a loop. Yrh and pull through all three loops on hook

dc3tog: double crochet 3 together decrease: *Insert hook into first st, yrh, pull through a loop. Without finishing st, rep from * into each of next 2 sts. Yrh and pull yarn through all four loops on hook

rep: repeat

Rnd(s): round, rounds

ss: slip stitch

st(s): stitch, stitches

yrh: yarn round hook

MATERIALS

- Small amount of No.5 crochet cotton, such as DMC Petra No.5 100% cotton, in bright blue (A) and light blue (B)
- 1.5mm (US size 8) steel crochet hook
- 1 x pair 6mm (¼ in.) safety eyes
- Toy stuffing
- Sewing needle
- Black embroidery thread

HEAD AND BODY

Using A, make 6dc in magic circle, pull tail to close.

Rnd 1: 2dc in each dc. (12 sts)

Rnd 2: *1dc in next dc, 2dc in next dc; rep from * to end. (18 sts)

Rnd 3: *1dc in each of next 2 dc, 2dc in next dc; rep from * to end. (24 sts)

Rnds 4–6: 1dc in each dc. (24 sts)

Rnd 7: *1dc in each of next 3 dc, 2dc in next dc; rep from * to end. (30 sts)

Rnds 8–10: 1dc in each dc. (30 sts)

Insert safety eyes and secure.

Rnd 11: *1dc in each of next 8 dc, dc2tog; rep from * to end. (27 sts)

Rnd 12: *1dc in each of next 7 dc, dc2tog; rep from * to end. (24 sts)

Rnd 13: *1dc in each of next 6 dc, dc2tog; rep from * to end. (21 sts)

Rnd 14: *1dc in each of next 5 dc, dc2tog; rep from * to end. (18 sts)

Rnd 15: *1dc in each of next 4 dc, dc2tog; rep from * to end. (15 sts)

Rnd 16: *1dc in each of next 3 dc, dc2tog; rep from * to end. (12 sts)

Stuff firmly.

Rnd 17: *1dc in each of next 2 dc, dc2tog; rep from * to end. (9 sts)

Rnd 18: *1dc in next dc, dc2tog; rep from * to end. (6 sts)

Rnd 19: Dc2tog around. (3 sts)

Fasten off, leaving a long tail.

SIDE FLIPPERS (MAKE 2)

Using A, make 4dc in magic circle, pull tail to close.

Rnd 1: *1dc in next dc, 2dc in next dc; rep from * once more. (6 sts)

Rnd 2: 2dc in each dc. (12 sts)

Rnds 3–5: 1dc in each dc. (12 sts)

Rnd 6: 1dc in next dc, dc2tog; rep from * to end. (8 sts)
Fasten off, leaving a long tail.

BACK FIN (MAKE 2 HALVES)

Using A, ch6.
Row 1: Miss 1 ch, 1dc in each of next 5 chs, turn. (5 sts)
Row 2: Ch1, 1dc in each dc, turn.
Row 3: Ch1, dc2tog, 1dc in next dc, dc2tog, turn. (3 sts)
Row 4: Ch1, dc3tog, turn.
Row 5: Ch1, 1dc in dc.
Fasten off, leaving a long tail.

TAIL FINS (MAKE 2)

Using A, make 4dc in magic circle, pull tail to close
Rnd 1: *1dc in next dc, 2dc in next dc; rep from * once more. (6 sts)
Rnd 2: *1dc in next dc, 2dc in next dc; rep from * to end. (9 sts)
Rnd 3: 1dc in each dc. (9 sts)
Ss in next dc and fasten off, leaving a long tail.

BELLY

Using B, ch8.
Rnd 1: Miss 1 ch, 3dc in next ch, 1dc in each of next 5 chs, 3dc in last ch. Working down other side of ch, 1dc in each of next 5 chs.
Rnd 2: *2dc in each of next 3 dc, 1dc in each of next 5 dc; rep from * once more.
Rnd 3: *[1dc in next dc, 2dc in next dc] 3 times, 1dc in each of next 5 dc; rep from * once more.
Ss in next st and fasten off, leaving a long tail.

FINISHING

Use yarn end to close hole in body. Sew open edge of side flippers to sides of body.
Sew two halves of back fin together with whipstitch, stuffing lightly. Leave one long yarn end and use to sew fin to back of body.
Use yarn ends to sew open edge of tail fins to either side of point at end of body, as shown, and to sew belly to bottom of body.
Embroider mouth in black embroidery thread.

FINISHED SIZES

Dolphin: 5cm (2 in.) long, 4cm (1½ in.) tall to top of fin

Annabelle the Doll

Annabelle is eight years old. She adores pretty dresses, but also loves climbing trees, so her mum is always having to mend her dresses and put plasters on scraped knees. Annabelle likes having long hair, even though she has to tie it back most of the time so she can go on her adventures.

HEAD AND BODY
Using A make 6dc in magic circle. Pull tail to close.

Rnd 1: 2dc in each dc. (12 sts)

Rnds 2–6: 1dc in each dc. (12 sts)

Rnd 7: Dc2tog around. (6 sts)

Rnd 8: 2dc in each dc. (12 sts)

Rnds 9–13: 1dc in each dc. (12 sts)

Stuff firmly.

Rnd 14: Dc2tog around. (6 sts)

Fasten off, leaving a long tail for sewing.

ARMS AND LEGS (MAKE 4)
Using A, make 5dc in magic circle.

Rnds 1–3: 1dc in each dc.

Fasten off, leaving a long tail for sewing.

DRESS
Using B, ch21, join with ss into ring.

Rnds 1–4: Ch1, 1dc in each dc.

Change to C.

Rnd 5: Working in front loop only, *ss in next st, ch2; rep from * to end.

ABBREVIATIONS
ch(s): chain, chains

dc: double crochet

dc2tog: double crochet 2 together decrease. Insert hook in next st, yrh, pull through a loop. Without finishing st, insert hook in next st, yrh and pull through a loop. Yrh and pull through all three loops on hook

htr: half treble

rep: repeat

Rnd(s): round, rounds

ss: slip stitch

st(s): stitch, stitches

yrh: yarn round hook

MATERIALS
Doll
- ¼ x ball, approx 25m (27 yds), of DK (light worsted) cotton, such as Knit Picks CotLin 70% cotton/30% linen, in pale beige (A)
- 2.0mm (US size 4) steel crochet hook
- Toy stuffing
- Sewing needle
- Oddments of 6-strand embroidery thread in red and bright blue
- Small amount of No.5 crochet cotton, such as DMC Petra No.5 100% cotton, in yellow (D)

Dress
- Oddments of No.5 crochet cotton, such as DMC Petra No.5 100% cotton, in pink (B) and blue (C)
- 1.5mm (US size 8) steel crochet hook
- Sewing needle

Doll: 7.5cm (3 in.) tall

Rnd 6: Ch1, 1dc in back loop of dc from Round 4 around, ss in first dc to close.

Rnd 7: Ch2, 4htr in same st, *miss 2 sts, 5htr in next st (htr cluster made); rep from * to end, ss in top of first ch-2.

Rnd 8: Ss to third st of first htr cluster, ch2, 4htr in same st, *5htr in third st of next htr cluster; rep from * to end, ss in top of first ch-2 to close.

Fasten off, weave in ends.

STRAPS FOR DRESS (MAKE 2)

Using B, ch11, miss first ch, 1dc in each ch.

Fasten off, leaving a long tail.

FINISHING

Use yarn end to close hole in doll. Embroider face on doll using red and bright blue embroidery thread. Sew arms and legs to body.

For hair, cut 15cm (6 in.) lengths of D. Insert hook in top of head, fold one length of yarn in half over hook, and pull through to form a loop, then pull cut ends through loop. Trim to length when all hair has been inserted. Arrange hair in two bunches and tie with a length of bright blue embroidery thread.

Sew straps to dress bodice. Put dress on doll.

Stanley the Snail

This little snail is remarkably easy to make, as the wool does all the work to create the pattern! There are many beautiful self-striping sock wools available – why not make a family of snails in several colourways?

SNAIL

BODY
Using A, make 6dc in magic circle, pull tail to close.

Rnd 1: 2dc in each dc. (12 sts)

Rnds 2–36: 1dc in each dc. (12 sts) Insert safety eyes and secure. Stuff final 7 rounds only.

Rnd 37: Dc2tog around. (6 sts) Fasten off, leaving a long tail.

ANTENNAE (MAKE 2)
Using A, ch7, miss 1 ch, 1dc in each of next 6 chs. (6 sts) Fasten off, leaving a long tail.

FINISHING
Use yarn end to close hole in snail. Sew antennae to head.

Coil other end to form a shell and sew in place.

LEAF (MAKE 1 IN EACH COLOUR)
Ch11, miss 1 ch, 1dc in next ch, *1htr in next ch, 1tr in each of next 2 ch, 1dtr in each of next 2 ch, 1tr in each of next 2 ch, 1htr in next ch**, 3dc in last ch. Working down other side of ch; rep from * to **, 2dc in last ch, ss in first dc. Fasten off.

FINISHING
Weave in ends.

FINISHED SIZES

Snail: 4cm (1½ in.) tall
Leaf: 4.5cm (1¾ in.) long

LITTLE *Ladybirds*

Alice and Edith have been friends since they hatched from their tiny eggs. They like to spend time on the same leaf, munching on aphids and chatting about their ladybird adventures.

LADYBIRD

BODY
Using A, make 6dc into magic circle, pull tail to close.
Rnd 1: 2dc in each dc. (12 sts)
Rnds 2–3: 1dc in each dc. (12 sts)
Ss in first dc to join, cut yarn and fasten off.

BASE
Using B, ch5, miss first ch, 1dc in next ch, 1htr in each of next 2 chs, 3dc in last ch.
Working down other side of ch, 1htr in each of next 2 chs, 1dc in next ch. Fasten off, leaving long tail for sewing.

FACE
Using B, make 4dc into magic circle, pull tail to close.
Rnd 1: 2dc in each dc. (8 sts)
Cut yarn, leaving a long tail for sewing.
Fasten off.

FINISHING
Tuck yarn ends inside body to act as stuffing. Sew base of ladybird to body with whip st.
Use B to embroider French knots as spots. Using C, embroider eyes on face. Sew face to front of body with whip st.

LEAF
Using D, ch22.
Rnd 1: Ss in second ch, *1htr in each of next 4 chs, 1tr in each of next 4 chs, 1dtr in each of next 4 chs, 1tr in each of next 4 chs, 1htr in each of next 4 chs**, ss in same st as last htr. Working down other side of ch; rep from * to **, join with ss in first ss.
Rnd 2: *1htr in each of 4 htr, 1tr in each of 4 tr, 2dtr in each of 4 dtr, 1tr in each of 4 tr, 1htr in each of 4 htr**, ss in ss; rep from * to **, join with ss in first ss.
Fasten off.

MATERIALS
Ladybirds
- Oddments of 6-strand cotton embroidery thread in red (A), black (B) and white (C)
- 1.5mm (US size 8) steel crochet hook
- Sewing needle

Leaf
- Oddments of 4-ply (fingering) cotton, such as Rowan Summerlite 4-ply 100% cotton, in green (D)
- 2.0mm (US size 4) steel crochet hook

FINISHED SIZES
Ladybird: 1.5cm (⅔ in.) long
Leaf: 7.5cm (3 in.) long

NOTES
You could also use the leaf with a crocheted flower to make a brooch, or sew several leaves to another crochet project as embellishment.

FUZZY *Caterpillar*

Clive the fuzzy caterpillar spends all day on his leaf, munching slowly around the edges until he's had his fill. He's hoping to grow a few more segments, so he makes sure to eat as much as possible. Clive can be posed in a variety of positions thanks to the fine wire that runs through his segments.

CATERPILLAR SEGMENTS (MAKE 2 OR MORE IN EACH COLOUR)

Make 6dc in magic circle, pull tail to close.

Rnd 1: 2dc in each dc. (12 sts)

Rnd 2: *1dc in next dc, 2dc in next dc; rep from * to end. (18 sts)

Rnds 3–5: 1dc in each dc. (18 sts)

Rnd 6: *1dc in next dc, dc2tog; rep from * to end. (12 sts)

Turn so fuzzier side is facing out and stuff firmly.

Rnd 7: Dc2tog around. (6 sts)

Cut yarn, leaving a long tail. Thread through rem sts and pull tight to close.

FINISHING

Thread all segments onto a length of yarn and secure. Fold a double length of wire in half and push through all segments, allowing the ends to form the antennae.

ABBREVIATIONS

dc: double crochet

dc2tog: double crochet 2 together decrease. Insert hook in next st, yrh, pull through a loop. Without finishing st, insert hook in next st, yrh and pull through a loop. Yrh and pull through all three loops on hook

rem: remaining

rep: repeat

Rnd(s): round, rounds

st(s): stitch, stitches

yrh: yarn round hook

MATERIALS

- Small amounts of laceweight yarn, such Rowan Kidsilk Haze 70% mohair/30% silk, in green and pink
- 1.5mm (US size 8) steel crochet hook
- Toy stuffing
- Sewing needle
- Short length of fine craft wire (optional)

FINISHED SIZES

Caterpillar: approx 6cm (2⅓ in.) long

NOTES

Make the caterpillar longer for younger children to avoid any danger of choking. Do not add the wire if the caterpillar is for a younger child, as it may cause a scratch.

BASIC *Techniques*

HOLDING THE HOOK

Hold the hook in the dominant hand either like a knife or like a pencil, as shown. Both holds are correct so use whichever feels most comfortable.

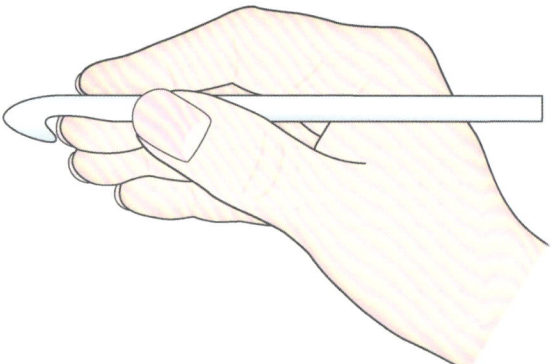

Holding the book like a pencil

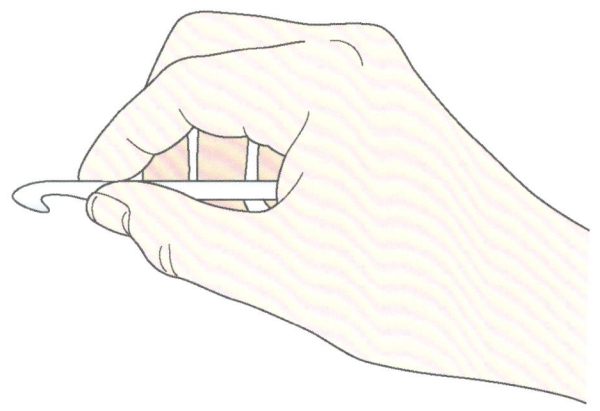

Holding the hook like a knife

HOLDING THE YARN

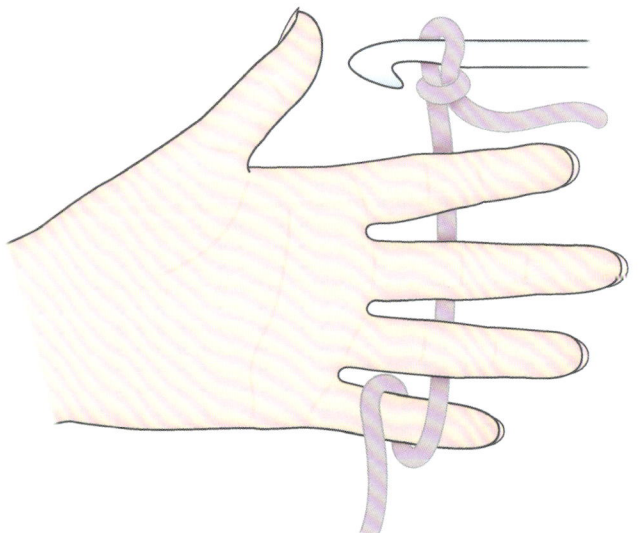

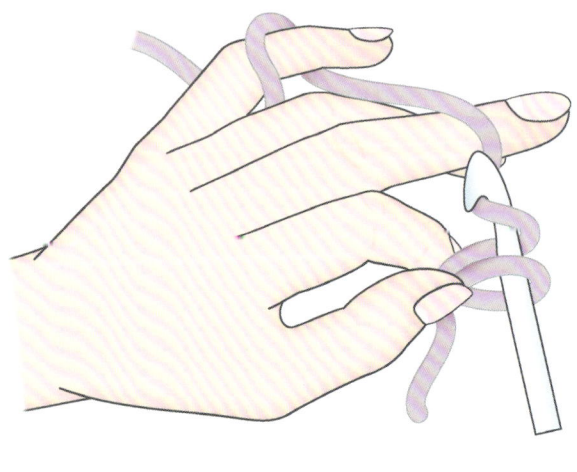

On the non-dominant hand, wrap the yarn around the little finger, then across the back of the other fingers – or take it over the palm side of the ring finger, and back of middle and first finger, whichever feels most comfortable.

Lift the middle finger to tension the yarn and hold the work with the first finger and thumb, as illustrated above. Alternatively, lift the first finger to tension the yarn and hold the work with the middle finger and thumb.

YARN ROUND HOOK (YRH)

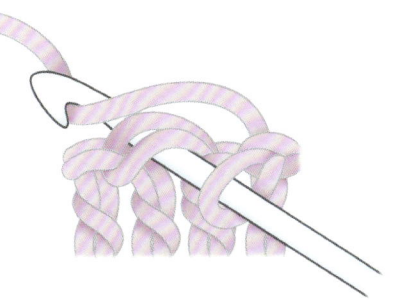

Also known as yarn over (yo), or sometimes yarn over hook (yoh). The hook should always swing under the tensioned yarn, toward the back.

SLIP STITCH (SS)

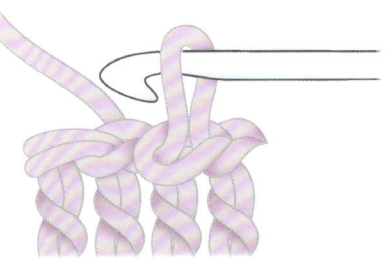

1. Insert the hook into the stitch or chain required, yarn round hook.

2. Pull through both work AND loop on hook without yarning over again. One slip stitch made.

CROCHET STITCH CONVERSION CHART

Crochet stitches are worked in the same way in both the UK and the USA, but the stitch names are not the same and identical names are used for different stitches. Below is a list of the UK terms used in this book, and the equivalent US terms.

UK term	US term
double crochet (dc)	single crochet (sc)
half treble (htr)	half double crochet (hdc)
treble (tr)	double crochet (dc)
double treble (dtr)	treble (tr)
triple treble (ttr)	double treble (dtr)
quadruple treble (qtr)	triple treble (ttr)
tension	gauge
yarn round hook (yrh)	yarn over hook (yoh)

MAKING A CHAIN (CH)

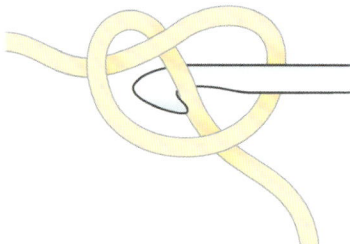 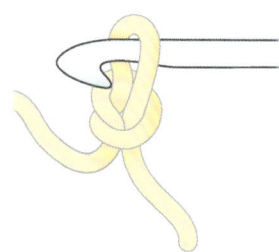 

1. Start with a slip knot; make a loop in the yarn, insert the hook and catch the back strand.

2. Pull the yarn through to make a loop, then gently pull on both ends to close the loop on the hook.

3. Hold the slip knot with the non-dominant hand and push the hook forward and under the tensioned yarn, catching the yarn, then pull the yarn through the loop on the hook. One chain made.

DOUBLE CROCHET (DC)

1. Insert the hook into the stitch or chain required. Yarn round hook and pull up a loop (2 loops on hook).

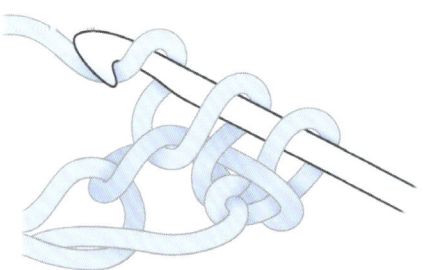

2. Yarn round hook again and pull through both loops on the hook. One double crochet made.

HALF TREBLE (HTR)

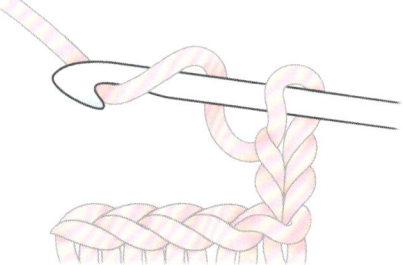

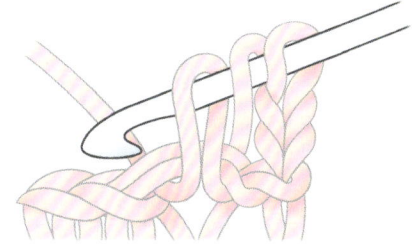

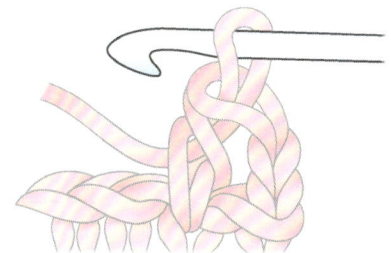

1. Yarn round hook first, then insert the hook into the stitch or chain required.

2. Yarn round hook and pull up a loop (3 loops on hook).

3. Yarn round hook and pull through all three loops on the hook. One half-treble made.

TREBLE (TR)

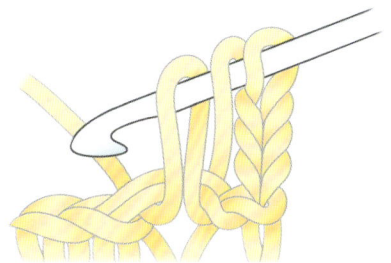

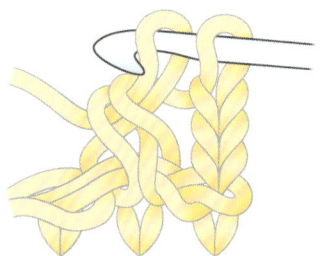

1. Yarn round hook first, then insert the hook into the stitch or chain required. Yarn round hook and pull up a loop (3 loops on hook).

2. Yarn round hook and pull through two loops on the hook (2 loops on hook).

3. Yarn round hook, pull through the last two loops on the hook. One treble made.

DOUBLE TREBLE (DTR)

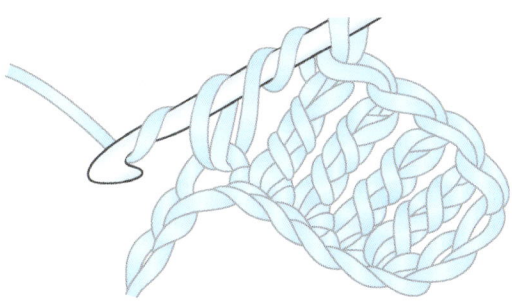

Yarn round hook twice first, then insert the hook into the stitch or chain required. Yarn round hook and pull up a loop, yarn round hook and pull through two loops, yarn round hook and pull through two loops again, yarn round hook and pull through the last two loops on the hook. One double-treble made.

DOUBLE CROCHET 2 TOGETHER (DC2TOG)

1. Insert the hook into the next stitch, yarn round hook, pull up a loop, then insert the hook into the next stitch.

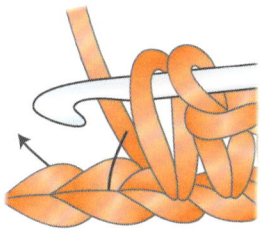

2. Yarn round hook and pull up a loop, yarn round hook and pull through all three loops on the hook. One double crochet 2 together decrease made.

HALF TREBLE 2 TOGETHER (HTR2TOG)

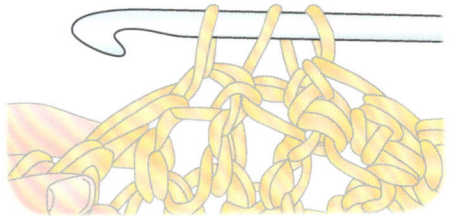

1. Yarn round hook, insert the hook into the next stitch, yarn round hook and pull up a loop (3 loops on hook).

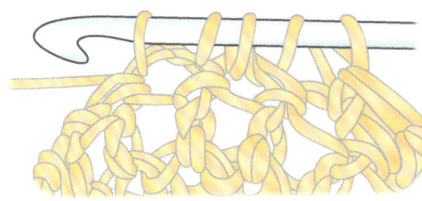

2. Yarn round hook, insert the hook into the next stitch, yarn round hook and pull up a loop (5 loops on hook).

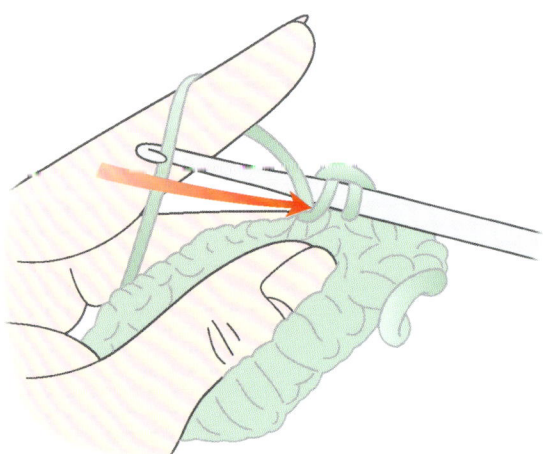

3. Yarn round hook and pull through all five loops on the hook. One half-treble 2 together decrease made. Treble 2 together (tr2tog), is worked using the same basic technique (see page 21 for written instructions).

LOOP DOUBLE CROCHET (LPDC)

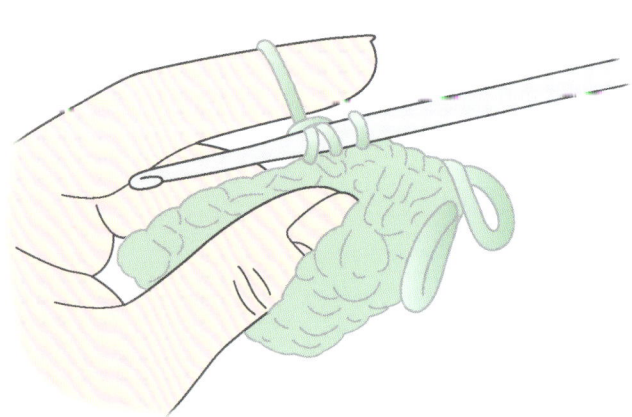

1. Insert the hook into the stitch required, yarn round hook with BOTH PIECES of yarn held over your tensioning finger, then pull through.

2. Adjust loop to the size desired, then finish the stitch. One loop double crochet stitch made.

MAGIC CIRCLE TECHNIQUE

This is also sometimes called magic/adjustable/slip ring or magic/adjustable/loop.

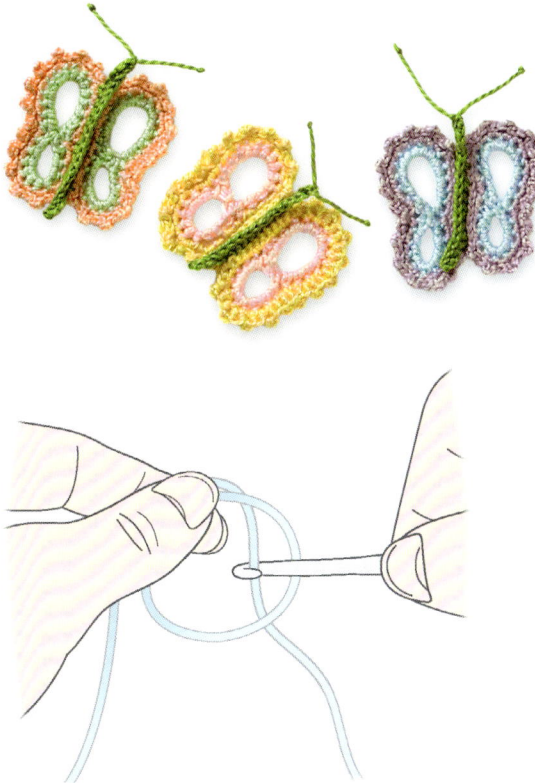

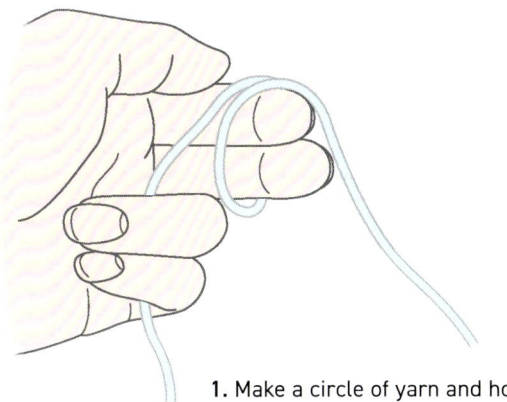

1. Make a circle of yarn and hold as shown.

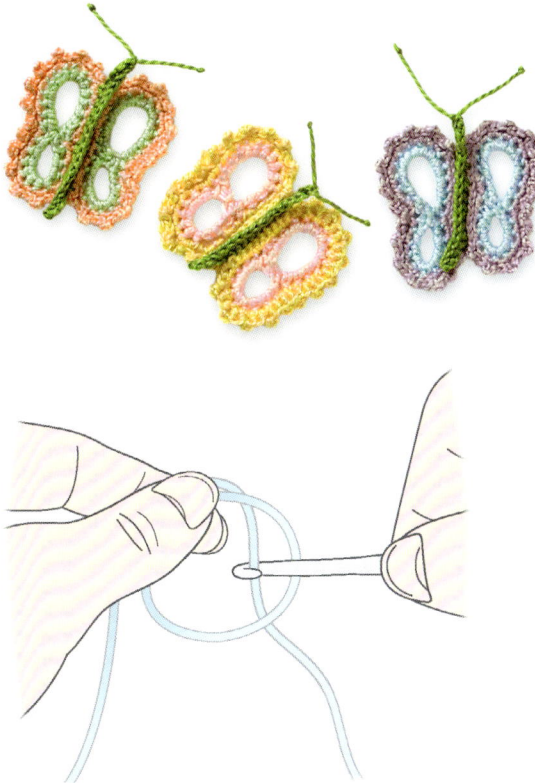

2. Insert the hook into the circle, pull the active yarn through then make a chain.

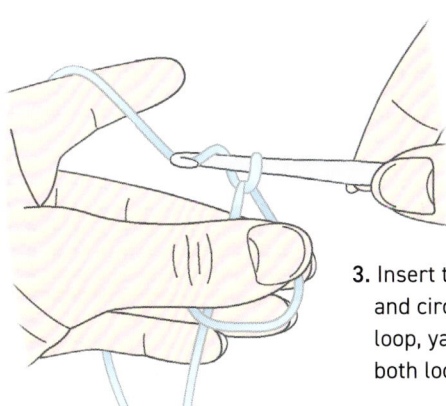

3. Insert the hook into the circle (under both tail and circle side), yarn round hook and pull up a loop, yarn round hook again and pull through both loops on hook to make a double crochet.

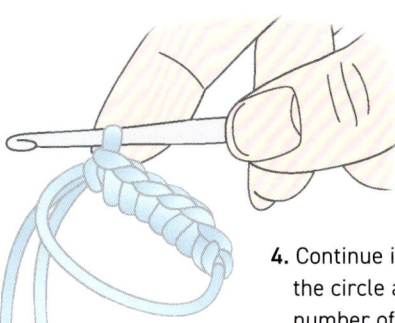

4. Continue inserting the hook into the circle and make the required number of double crochet stitches.

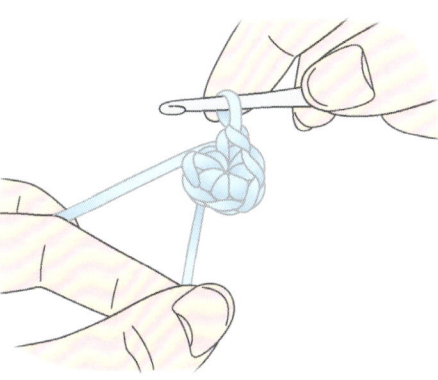

5. Once you have made the required number of stitches, pull on the tail to close the circle (make sure the tail is free to pull and not wrapped round the circle).

FASTENING (FINISHING) OFF CROCHET

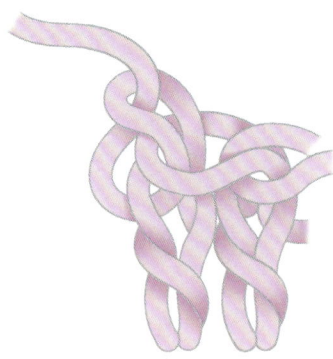

1. Cut the yarn, leaving a minimum 10cm (4 in.) tail – leave longer for projects requiring a long tail.

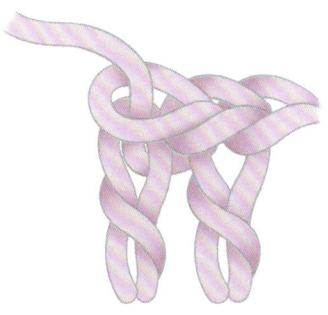

2. Pull the tail all the way through the remaining loop on the hook to secure the end.

WORKING IN CONTINUOUS SPIRAL ROUNDS

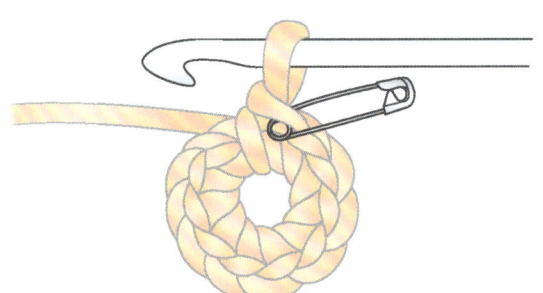

A chain is not necessary at the beginning of the round, and a slip stitch is not necessary at the end of the round. A new round will be started in the first stitch of the previous round. Use a stitch marker of some kind, such as a small safety pin as shown here, to mark the first stitch of the round.

WORKING INTO FRONT OR BACK LOOP OF STITCH

Unless the pattern instructs you to use the front loop or the back loop, you should always insert your hook under both legs of the V of each stitch when crocheting.

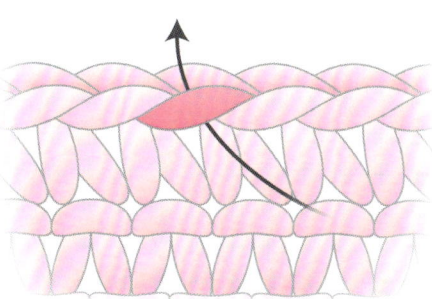

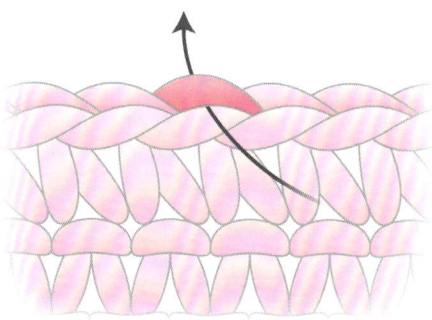

Front loop The front loop is the leg nearest to you. To work into the front loop of a stitch, pick up the front loop from underneath at the front of the work.

Back loop The back loop is the leg further away from you. To work into the back loop of the stitch, insert the hook between the front and the back loop, picking up the back loop from the front of the work.

AROUND THE POST STITCH

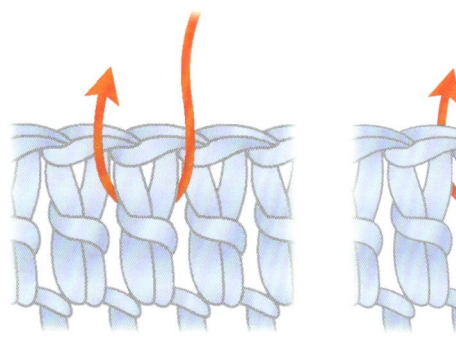
Front post stitch

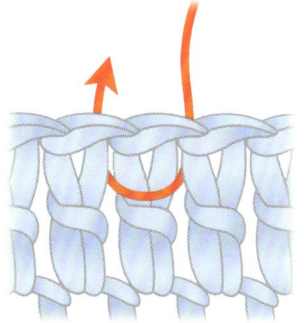
Back post stitch

Instead of inserting the hook into the V of the required stitch, insert it around the vertical part (the post) of the stitch from the row below.

DOUBLE CROCHET JOIN

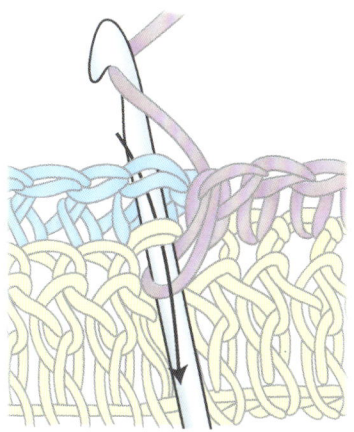

Insert the hook through both stitches to be joined, yarn over and pull up a loop, yarn over and pull through both loops on the hook.

Embroidery

FRENCH KNOTS

Bring the needle through to the front of the work. Wrap the thread around the needle once, twice or three times depending on the size of knot desired, then insert the needle back into the work, very close to the original spot. Pull the wraps tight so they rest against the surface of the work, then pull the needle through to the back.

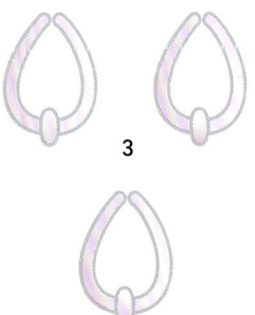

BACK STITCH

Bring the needle through to the front of the work. Take the needle to the back of the work to make a stitch the length desired (usually 0.5cm/¼ in.), then go forward a stitch length and bring the yarn through to the front of the work again. Go back to the end of the first stitch made and take the needle to the back. Repeat as required.

LAZY DAISY STITCH

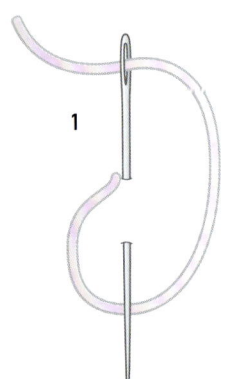

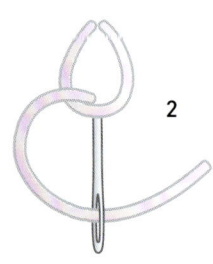

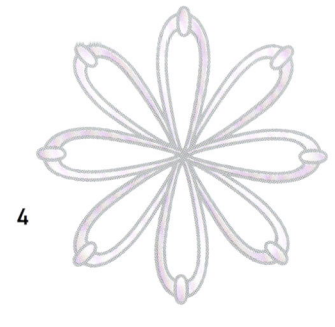

Bring the needle to the front of the work. Insert it into the same hole and, in the same motion, bring the needle back out a petal-length away (1) and loop the thread around

the tip (2). Take the needle to the back of the work on the other side of the loop, securing it, and bring back out in the centre (3). Continue around in a circle until a daisy is made (4).

USEFUL *Websites*

DMC
www.dmc.com

COATS CRAFTS
www.coatscrafts.co.uk

ROWAN YARNS
www.knitrowan.com

BLACK SHEEP WOOLS
www.blacksheepwools.com

YARNSTICK
www.yarnstick.co.uk

PURPLELINDA CRAFTS
www.purplelindacrafts.co.uk

LOVECRAFTS
www.lovecrafts.com

WOOL WAREHOUSE
www.woolwarehouse.co.uk

If you wish to accurately substitute a different yarn for one recommended in a pattern, try the Yarnsub website for suggestions: www.yarnsub.com

I also recommend exploring your local yarn stores to support small business owners and see what treasures you might find.

Acknowledgements

I am so grateful to everyone who helped make this book possible. Cindy Richards and Gillian Haslam at CICO Books made this project happen and were incredibly kind to me; thank you both. Many thanks to my fab editor Marie Clayton for being eagle-eyed and patient. Trina Dalziel created the beautiful sets for photography and Geoff Dann took the brilliant photos; thank you both for your vision. My beloved late grandmother, Catherine Jane, taught me to crochet when I was seven years old, which was the greatest gift she could have given me. Finally, I want to thank my husband Julian for his infinite patience, support, encouragement and love.

Index